THE RIGHT THING

THE RIGHT THING

ethics inaction
or
ethics in action

by

William D. Brown, Ph.D

The Wayne Smith Company
Washington, DC

Brown, William D. (William David), 1936 -
        The Right Thing: ethics inaction or ethics in action

        Bilbliography and Index: p.
        1. Ethics (Personal)   2. Ethics (Business)   3. Values   I.
Title.

Library of Congress Catalog Card Number: 91-66190

ISBN 0-9630610-1-1

Inquiries and order requests should be addressed to:

        The Wayne Smith Company
        1300 L Street, N.W.
        Suite 1050
        Washington, DC 20005
        (202)484-5620

Jacket Design by Ed Miller

Dedication

In memory and honor of all who have served and who will serve as good role models for you.

And in honor of you, as you strive daily to be a good role model for those you influence.

Books by William D. Brown

Two roads diverged in a wood, and I ---

I took the one less traveled by,

And that has made all the difference.

from
Robert Frost
"The Road Not Taken"

Table of Contents

ACKNOWLEDGEMENTS

No book is ever the singular effort of a lone author. Rather, any work must be attributed to all who helped assist the writer in the growth process of becoming.

When I think back over the lives that have influenced mine, the list is endless. Suffice it to say that every door that was ever opened for me was the result of the efforts of someone who cared and who went the extra mile to help me succeed. My gratitude is especially extended to my parents, brothers and sisters, and all relatives for their encouragement. Certainly this also applies to many good friends.

An earlier book dedication to my best friend, my wife, read:

"To Nett on whose bright disposition
the sun will never set."

That it hasn't throughout the trials of writing this book is cause for me to be forever grateful.

Finally, it is with a note of special appreciation to Jim Goode, Chris and Sharon Hough, Susan Kris, Bob Phillips, Virginia Taylor, Barney and Joanne Thomas, and Mary Jane Young, each of whom assisted in helping to bring The Right Thing to fruition. Thanks!

PREFACE

The Right Thing: ethics inaction or ethics in action. This book has as its ---

Mission: To raise the quality of life by helping readers think through and reflect on the outcome of choosing the harder right over the easier wrong in decision making.

Purpose: To help guide anyone capable of determining right from wrong to make better decisions.

Goal: To have an impact for good throughout society, by influencing us positively in our (1) personal, (2) interpersonal, and (3) business lives.

Audience: The intended audience consists of students striving to live quality lives who have yet to embark on careers where many difficult choices will be encountered; military personnel of all ranks who must think and act ethically before they can successfully lead or be led; family members and friends who seek greater satisfaction in their relationships, and, of course, persons in business who sense that in the long run only persons and businesses that strive to do The Right Thing will prosper and survive on the brink of the 21st century.

A book for all people? No. Rather it is intended for those who sense the benefits to be derived from focused living, not on ethics inaction, but rather on **ethics in action.**

<u>Consider</u>: "Would your life be better today had you always listened to your conscience and chosen to do <u>The Right Thing</u>?" Doesn't it follow then that future quality of life will be better for those who actively choose the harder right over the easier wrong?

Whether a parent, child, spouse, employee, employer, mid-manager, executive, or entrepreneur --- truly there is no time like the present to consider

<u>The Right Thing</u>
<u>ethics inaction or ethics in action</u>

as it affects the whole fabric of life.

William D. Brown
Washington, DC
Fall, 1991

INTRODUCTION

Give your immediate response to the following questions:

<u>True</u> <u>False</u>

 1. Doing <u>The Right Thing</u> is relatively simple for people with highly developed consciences.

2. Consideration of <u>The Right Thing</u> would possibly help people in jail or those who have never been taught right from wrong, but it would hardly be of much help to me.

☐ ☐ 3. Once a high ethical code has been adopted, most people will choose <u>The Right Thing</u> when making decisions.

☐ ☐ 4. Deciding on <u>and</u> executing what is right in daily choices is not something that can be taught, but, rather is something to be caught by exposure to others doing what is right.

☐ ☐ 5. Some individuals live by such high ethical codes that any discussion of <u>The Right Thing</u> seems unnecessary or at best mindful of the proverbial case of carrying coals to Newcastle.

<u>Item # 1: False</u>

Doing what is right is often easier said than done. One can't rest on past ethical conduct. Temptation is constant. Only when we give prior thought to doing what is right and diligently apply high ethical principles to all decisions do we stand a chance of leading principled lives.

Some people with highly developed consciences nonetheless continually exceed posted speed limits. That they would never think of stealing is a given. They know such is wrong. However, little thought is given to excessive highway speed, underscoring once again that a highly developed conscience is an elusive goal unless pursued relentlessly.

Ethics (properly used interchangeably in the singular or plural) is a way of life, not a set of absolute principles. Nor does the topic suggest a regimented way of thinking. Rather, ethics serves as a strong connecting link between endless adjustments and constant compromises.

Item # 2: False

Consideration of what is right will assist anyone approaching the subject with an open mind. Those who have done wrong (incarcerated or still on the streets) certainly would benefit from reflecting and meditating on The Right Thing. But which of us wouldn't?

The field of politics hardly fails to disappoint when seeking examples of principled men and women who occasionally falter. The Senator, commonly perceived both by others as well as presumably by his family and himself as a person of integrity, was embarrassed and shamed when his involvement with a woman, younger than one of his daughters, was revealed. The phrase "feet of clay" too often describes not only the famous but the rest of us as well.

In fact, temptations to choose the expedient thing over the right thing confront us daily. The "Don't Walk" signs at busy corners, the red stoplight late at night when presumably no one is around, are both tests of our ethical development. Ethical awareness helps to keep us mindful that we are intricately bound as part of a natural order. Interests of others are invariably and inevitably tied to our own.

Item # 3: False

Codes of ethics must be continually built. There is nothing static about choosing to do what is right. True, good decisions made yesterday have a bearing on judgments exercised today, but ethics will never remain of a high order without a great expenditure of effort. Unless we remain vigilant, it is easy to rationalize, finding an excuse to be less than ethical "just this once."

The other morning while heading to a local seminar I had to stop briefly by my Washington office. "No Parking" signs proliferate on Connecticut Avenue during this hour. On top of that, a police cruiser was parked in the middle of the block. Still, I wouldn't be but three minutes. . .

. . .so, pulling in front of the officer, I cut off the ignition, put on the emergency flashers, and raised the hood where I jiggled something momentarily before running inside. Hardly a pronouncement of car trouble, the act did <u>insinuate</u> that I was experiencing an engine problem.

Returning shortly, I slammed the hood shut, started the car, and drove off. Only while driving away, contemplating the cleverness of this maneuver, were the ethical implications weighed. And this by one actively writing a book entitled <u>The Right Thing: ethics inaction or ethics in action</u>!

Ethical decisions will not be made just because a high ethical code is in place. Application must be constant if we are to continue enjoying the fruits of having exercised a higher order ethical decision.

<u>Item # 4: False</u>

Making ethical decisions is a skill that can be both <u>taught</u> and <u>caught</u>. Appealing to reason is an effective means of teaching nearly anyone of normal or higher intelligence. During the early years of this country ethics were instilled in young children in schoolrooms across the land via the almost universal use of the famed McGuffey readers.

In <u>The Eclectic First Reader for Young Children</u>, McGuffey included a story entitled "The Cruel Boy", where six year old George, who had been bad, was made to feel sorrowful, with the hope that he would not be mischievous in the future. George's fairly well-developed conscience is assumed. Given what we know of the present weakened family structure often with so few good role models, is such an assumption prudent today?

If ethics is neither instilled nor taught well in many homes, neither is the subject inculcated as a general rule in today's students. In fact in many classroom settings ethics are not mentioned at all, with the implication that somehow ethical material can't or shouldn't be taught. But there is no escaping the reality that ethics can be instilled through teaching.

Concurrently, ethics are daily <u>caught</u> by each of us as we witness people making ethical decisions. The more esteem in which one acting ethically is held, the greater the impact their ethical decision-making will have on us. Ethics both <u>taught</u> and <u>caught</u>? But of course!

Item # 5: False

Remaining ever vigilant in making sound ethical decisions requires both study and application. It is not enough to want to lead a good life: we must apply ourselves to this end without faltering if we are to succeed when decision time arrives, affording us little opportunity to weigh the pros and cons of required judgments.

In the military, where decision-making is

confronted constantly during field exercises, leaders are aware of the necessity of instilling and inculcating desired values to such an extent that they can count on themselves to choose instinctively the harder right over the easier wrong. But again, this doesn't come about by osmosis or by having long ago given extensive thought to ethical decision making. Rather, the best assurance that the end result of our reasoning will culminate in ethical decisions is to be found in those men and women who have consciously chosen to think and respond ethically in all that they do. Matters big and small will have undergone [and be undergoing] constant ethical scrutiny, with the realization that actions affecting small things carry inordinate importance when major decisions must be made.

Recognizing there is no right way to do the wrong thing, we must be cautious that we not expect to benefit from <u>every</u> ethical decision made. Occasionally the immediate benefit will go to another. But consider the <u>long-term</u> advantage.

Periodically you may conclude that ethical decision making is not self-serving but is solely a means of doing good unto others. At these moments you need to remind yourself that ethical decision making allows you to look at yourself in the mirror without wincing, to be proud of the one you are becoming. It is a constant process.

Although throughout life ethics won't necessarily make the difference in the 100-yard dash, it <u>will</u> in the long-distance, cross-country run, which is of far greater importance than the payoff of the moment. For rather than isolated pride now it is your collective pride stemming from your numerous ethical decisions that will best help you in becoming the one you want to become.

So beginning with <u>The Right Thing</u> will prove beneficial. For ethical quandaries as carefully examined in each of the following three sections will cause you to draw on inner resources which may pleasantly surprise you. The positive impact resulting from such efforts will have a great influence for good on your future.

The odds, then, of your doing <u>The Right Thing</u> will increase significantly, especially as you refer repeatedly to the brief descriptions of selected ethical styles in Appendix A and apply the six criteria in Appendix B in deciding whether an action is ethical in each of the 30 case studies that follow.

Welcome then to this opportunity to grow in stature as you work at improving your ethical skills while considering

<u>The Right Thing</u>
<u>ethics inaction or ethics in action</u>

which will help position you well on an issue promising to represent tomorrow's cutting edge: **ethics**.

PART I.

Applying Ethics PERSONALLY

PART I.

"Applying Ethics PERSONALLY"

Are ideas of morality mere preferences (like one's taste for Zucchini)? Surely there is some agreement regarding the practice of ethics as applied personally.

Most people would concede that acts by the international shipping agent in White Plains, New York, who shipped animal feed instead of powdered milk to famine-stricken Sudan represents ethics inaction. The switch to the cheaper animal feed which resembles powdered milk but is not fit for human consumption was discovered by Sudanese officials, who alerted U. S. authorities.

What does this action suggest about the personal code of ethics subscribed to by the individual who made this decision? Taking advantage of persons or situations to reap personal gain is often the motivating factor leading to ethics inaction. Occasionally the culprit is a poorly developed conscience. In other cases the cause can either be attributed to a total lack of ethics or an ethical system run amuck. No matter. The result is usually the same: ethics inaction.

Sometimes a chief problem for rescuers at scenes of major accidents is not to care for the injured but to determine <u>who</u> has been injured. This surprising twist is due to bystanders recognizing an opportunity to parlay being in the right place at the right time into something big, like big money.

Fire fighters, police officers, and paramedics on the scene, report incidents where following a train collision within a station, people jumped from the other platform attempting to get <u>into</u> the wrecked train.

In another incident, columnist Mike Royko tells of two little old ladies being carried in a cab that was rear-ended. While the ladies sat and waited for help, bystanders who had been on the sidewalk jumped into the cab, holding their necks and moaning.

A similar occurrence took place in front of a tavern when a car broadsided a bus. Noted an official, "You never saw a tavern clear out like that.

They were coming out in droves and trying to get on the bus or lying down in the street. One minute they were all inside, sitting on bar stools and drinking. The next minute they were outside, flat on their backs, holding their necks and yelling, 'Whiplash, I got whiplash.'"

That greed is the genesis of much ethical inaction hardly needs elaboration even to the least street-wise element. Accounts of fraud investigations of individuals who have neglected developing their personal codes of ethics appear in newspapers almost daily. In one major east coast city investigators examine a businessman, an ally of former public officials, who is suspected of fraudulently billing the city for several years for oil and gasoline that was never delivered.

As ecology issues push to the forefront, on the west coast investigators start sifting through mounting evidence that some individuals have been guilty of siphoning off water from public resources for years, with astronomical losses accruing to municipalities.

Meanwhile in the midwest, Chicago, as do other cities, has people on its payroll who spend 100% of their time attempting to locate and identify welfare cheats. Nor does the south, upper-midwest, or northeast escape similar ethical abuse by individuals who have ignored developing personal codes of ethics that will keep them from running afoul of the law.

However, less we think personal gain or

greed is the sole reason for what might be considered ethical lapses, consider the Montana case involving what has come to be known as the "Angels of Mercy". Hospice nurses, rather than following regulated and cumbersome procedures when their dying patients' experienced pain almost beyond their ability to bear, stepped in and immediately administered prescription drugs to those suffering. Said one nurse, "That's the reason I went into nursing: to relieve suffering."

Charged with administering stashed drugs that had previously been prescribed over several months in attempting to alleviate their patients' pain, at least six nurses face disciplinary procedures, with the possibility of suspension or revocation of their licenses.

For now the controversy rages in and around Helena, Montana, where both accusers and supporters reside. Even lapel buttons have surfaced, emblazoned with the message "Free the Hospice Six." A medical ethicist from the University of Minnesota has weighed in, arguing that though the nurses might have broken the letter of the law, "they may well have honored the moral spirit of nursing."

The prosecutor states that the case is not about human pain and suffering. Rather "it's about violations of the Nursing Practices Act..." Others are concerned that if ignored, such actions could result in chaos in the health professions. Two sides to a complex issue, each calling on individuals to make ethical decisions affecting them --- and sometimes others --- personally.

Who's right? Who's wrong? A case of personal ethics, of course. But which position best represents ethics inaction? Which best reflects ethics in action?

Obviously the application of ethics isn't always easy but this is hardly reason to assume that integrity is an unaffordable luxury or that morality is mere preference. All of which brings about the inquiry, "Just what is ethical?"

Such queries aren't always aided by consultants specializing in ethical decision making. One expert described ethical behavior as a function within a context, claiming it is relative to a culture, an era, or even to the pressures exerted in a given job. When he argued further that standards are in such a constant state of flux, who in our society can decide what is right and what is wrong, an observer wryly noted: "One looks in vain in such talk for anything that would have prevented a person assisting in rounding up European victims during the Holocaust and helping place them aboard trains headed for Auschwitz and other equally infamous destinations."

The problem with approaching ethics personally within the context of moral relativism is that situations are viewed as problems to be solved as if no one has previously had to deal with similar issues. But of course this isn't so.

Still, we must wonder what role models children observe in their parents, employees in their employers, students in their teachers, subordinates in superiors, spouses in spouses, or even friends in friends? For there is no question but that chance encounters or messages dropped without warning into conversations, can and do have great impact on others. What is required is not only a recognition that we need to take care in addressing our own ethical development personally, but that we must remain cognizant of our influence on the personal ethical development of others. After all, it is our influence --- yours as well as mine, without exception --- that is keenly felt and has considerable impact.

Granted, much that surrounds making ethical decisions ultimately relies on judgment. Samuel Johnson recognized this when regarding truthfulness he noted, "There must always be some exceptions to the requirement for total veracity, else you would be obliged to assist the murderer who inquires which way his intended victim has gone."

Consider for a moment, "How Ethical Are You?" If you know a subordinate is right but that his position is not popular with your superiors, would you stand up and speak out for the subordinate? How far would you go (or have you gone) in advancing yourself at another's expense on or off the job? Do you carry your fair share of the workload on a given project? When participating in a community endeavor, are you likely to give yourself over to the task or do you look for others to carry the work-load, realizing that in the end all will receive credit for the completed job regardless of individual effort expended?

Personal ethics are observed in decisions which may be described as consequential as well as those we might think inconsequential, at least for the moment. For instance, at a buffet would you cut off and place on your plate the asparagus tips, leaving the stalks for others waiting in line behind you?

While dining in a Mexican restaurant would you reach under the pile of tortillas, take the warm, second one, leaving the cold, top tortilla for another guest?

Or similarly, when getting a newspaper from a vending machine, are you likely to take the second copy, leaving behind the more tattered top paper for the next customer?

What about traveling? One would look long and hard to find someone who would dispute that flying tourist but charging a client for first class would be other than a case of ethics inaction. However, when staying in hotels, is it right to take all the room's bath amenities --- soap, shampoo, lotion, sewing kits, shoe-shine mit --- figuring they're yours, paid for as part of the price of the room for the night? What about towels? Washcloths? Where do you draw the line?

Prominent cases of personal ethics inaction or ethics in action can be observed universally. Think back to the Watergate scandal that rocked the country in the early seventies, forcing, for the first time in our history, a President to resign in disgrace. Many political scientists and ethicists have examined and continue to study the matter. With increased access to tapes recorded in the Nixon White House, we can expect even more scholars to enter the fray in the future, frequently beginning by inquiring, "How could such a thing happen?"

Few persons would conclude that those who went to work in the new administration in 1969 came to Washington with larceny in their hearts. Nor were these individuals with dishonest or checkered pasts, else they would not have received clearances acceptable to those around the new president. After all, what administration in the making needs problems stemming from actions of bad actors and/or bad publicity at the outset?

Rather, administration officials who waded or who were drawn into the Watergate scandal were people who most likely inched their way toward unethical actions, first misleading, then rationalizing, and finally lying to themselves, as well as to others. This is a classical example of what Hannah Arendt must have had in mind when she noted, "The sad truth is that most evil is done by people who never make up their minds to be good or evil."

A study of The Right Thing: ethics inaction or ethics in action is apropos in applying ethics personally. Not that this or any other work will cause blatantly unethical people to suddenly start making ethical decisions. But The Right Thing can have tremendous impact on persons who are open to the realization that ethical living represents a journey, not a destination. What difference will such study and application make? Who really knows but can you afford <u>not</u> to find out?

Ethics --- choosing what is right --- begins with each of us PERSONALLY. Yet, in recent years it's a subject that has been avoided on many fronts. In fact, Paul Mok, an ethics consultant and president of Training Associates of Richardson, Texas, has compared talking about ethics with a discussion of sex education. In each case, most everyone agrees the mission is noble but there is a reluctance as to where to start or how to broach the subject.

Whoever is seated at the head of the table, be it within the family, at the head of an organization, or leading a volunteer effort, is the one clearly responsible to see that ethics is an acceptable topic of conversation. For in so doing the message is sent that it is not only permissible but even expected that the subject of ethics is appropriate at every existing opportunity.

And what affect will emphasis on ethics PERSONALLY have on higher level ethics, i.e., interpersonally and in one's business life? William S. Kanaga, former U. S. Chamber of Commerce Chairman, says, "I have a deep concern with the lack of impact in our daily business life of the deep roots our country has inherited from its Judeo-Christian beginnings. What I see is a breakdown in the home and in family training --- in community life and in many of the positive aspects of peer pressure. Our young men and women entering the business world are fed with a large dosage of cynicism about how to succeed. That cynicism comes not alone from disclosures in the media and from some blase peers ahead of them, but also from the teachings they receive on, and the influences of, the university campus."

Do we have a right to expect more support from institutions in helping shore up personal ethics? What about other institutional support for the advancement of ethical development? How much difference could such support make in helping people decide and act on what is right?

The Treadway Commission (actually the National Commission on Fraudulent Financial Reporting, chaired by James C. Treadway, Jr., executive vice president and general counsel of Paine Webber Incorporated), says Kanaga, "found in the cases they examined a breakdown in fundamentals --- an inability, lack of desire, or perhaps simply the lack of instinctive reaction to make a morally correct decision when selecting from a number of options."

So consider: does your approach to integrity influence others to respond with their best rather than their worst? Your answer will depend on how strong a code of ethics you apply PERSONALLY. For such is far more than admirable: it is essential to your personal ethical development, as Chapters 1 through 10 attest.

CHAPTER ONE

"What Price Honesty?"

Has lying become a necessary evil? Listen to Paul Fink, former head of the American Psychiatric Association, commenting on the difficulty many individuals have in getting health insurance coverage because they have been in therapy. Says he, "I don't believe that anyone in this day and age should tell the truth. The stigma is too great."

A psychologist agrees, contending that whether someone is seeking psychotherapy is no one else's business. Further, she counsels patients to lie, asserting, "I think anyone who answers 'Yes' to such questions on a form would be terribly naive."

This is a modern problem, not one earlier faced by insurers. When health insurance was first made available its purpose was to cover acute medical care. Today's health care policy often covers medical care of any type, leaving the insurance vendors subject to what they claim are huge expenditures. Thus the extensive inquiries when prospective policy holders apply for medical coverage.

The difficulty is one of risk for the insurance company, which is reluctant to underwrite former patients who have had any of a number of medical care procedures, contending this group represents a higher risk than that found in the general population.

Nor is the question, "What is the price of honesty?," limited to finding health insurance. The high school wrestler who is light for his weight class in the upcoming meet is advised by his coach to conceal lead weights in his gym shorts before weighing in for the pending match. He does and subsequently wins his match, but at what cost?

A small boy was given a piece of candy by a department store Santa Claus. Leaving Santa's lap, he inquired if he could have another to take to his brother. "Oh," said Santa, "do you have a brother at home?" Not wanting to be blatantly dishonest, the youngster replied, "No, but my sister does and her brother sure would be happy!"

A young female, recently graduated from a first rate college, has been offered a highly sought industry position. However, she has little money and would like to travel. An airline advertises it will fly potential flight attendants to its home base for job interviews. She signs up, knowing she won't accept the job if offered. Rather, she sees this as an opportunity for a free trip. To ask the question conversely, "What price her dishonesty?" What is the cost?

A reputation for honesty pays off in dramatic ways. Donald Douglas, founder of what later became McDonnell Douglas Aircraft, early established such a reputation for his company. Competing against Boeing to sell Eastern Airlines its first big jets, Douglas was told by Captain Eddie Rickenbacker, then head of Eastern, that his company's proposed specifications for Eastern's planned DC-8 were good in every area except noise suppression. Douglas was given one last chance to out-promise the competition on this feature.

After consulting with his engineers, Mr. Douglas reported back to Captain Rickenbacker that he did not feel he could guarantee further noise suppression. Rickenbacker is said to have answered, "I knew you couldn't. I merely wanted to see if you were still honest. You just got yourself an order for $165 million dollars worth of aircraft!"

How great the temptation must have been for Douglas to stretch the truth by promising to deliver a feature resolving a problem he could only hope his engineers would solve before the first aircraft was delivered. In the end, Douglas' company was rewarded <u>precisely</u> because their leader had remained true to an ethical code which placed a premium on honesty.

What price are you willing to pay to remain honest? Will Rogers once said, "I'd rather be the man who <u>bought</u> the Brooklyn Bridge than the man who sold it." Such a statement suggests volumes about one's integrity.

Exercise

1. What scenarios can you think of where it is to one's advantage to lie?

2. How high a price is <u>too high a price</u> to pay for remaining honest?

3. Should children be taught absolutes regarding honesty in their undertakings with others? If "Yes", what absolutes should be taught?

4. Do you believe taking undue advantage of another is as dishonest as stealing?

5. What is the highest price you ever paid for having been dishonest? What have been the long-term ramifications?

6. What difference do you perceive in being "sly" as opposed to being dishonest? Where do you draw the line?

7. Consider the ethical implications: "Would the person who knows you best be willing to play a hand of poker with you --- over the phone?"

CHAPTER TWO

"When Faced with Temptation"

"Video Stabilizer - Eliminates all video copyguards" reads the ad in a national publication. Though the reader is cautioned elsewhere in the copy that the product is intended "for private home use only", is there <u>anyone</u> who actually believes there is nothing wrong with foregoing copyright restrictions even when the copy is intended only for personal use?

Current prevailing opinion seemingly holds that an action is all right so long as no one gets hurt. Copying something for your own use is supposedly acceptable because (a) you will not profit financially from the action and (b) the copyright guardian isn't losing out because in any event, you wouldn't have bought the material. What then is the logic against copying?

Even more troublesome, "Isn't it stealing to acquire material illegally, i.e., in spite of a copyright, and <u>regardless</u> of its intended use?"

How many radar detectors have been sold with the appeal that use of these products will benefit drivers by enabling them to detect police radar, thereby avoiding being ticketed? One major company has now shifted from the offense to the defense in billing its product with the twin assertions: "Why radar makes mistakes. How to protect yourself."

Yet, exists there the ring of truth in assuming people buy radar detectors so they can further reduce their <u>legitimate</u> speed when police radar is detected in order to lower chances of being confused with another speeding vehicle showing up at the same time on the policeman's radar screen?

Ah, but temptations abound to test one's ethics. A broken electric meter that no longer registers current used in your home is not your fault. However, once aware of this problem what is your responsibility to the power company? When should the utility be called and informed of the problem? Or should it be left to the meter reader to discover when next reading your meter?

A new clerk on the job is befuddled and gives you a dollar too much while making change. Perhaps you would call the mistake to his attention, basking internally in having made the right choice. But would you respond similarly were there an error of five dollars in your favor? How about a $10 or $20 error? Would the amount make a difference?

Obviously the right answer is, "No," but for many the temptation grows in proportion to the size of the error. Thus we fall victim to a similar trap laid by George Bernard Shaw, when he reportedly asked a woman if she would spend the evening with him for a thousand dollars. Upon replying that she would have to think about it, she was asked if she would spend the evening with him for ten dollars? The woman upbraided the writer, replying, "Why Mr. Shaw, just what kind of woman do you think I am?"

Responded the wit, "Lady, we already settled that question. Now we are simply haggling over price."

Temptations abound in the work place for everyone, even when a high level of trust is assumed. Yet, how easily this level of trust is compromised. Consider the salesperson who has failed to meet quota --- again. He has a prospect who cannot qualify for credit but who is eager to own the product he sells. Peers in his sales organization brag how they can get "anybody" credit. The salesperson is well aware that such a method is both deceptive and dishonest. However, with but two phone calls --- one to a savvy peer who knows the ropes and the other to the customer to come down and sign on the dotted line --- the sales person will be above quota for the month, possibly saving his job.

What should he do? What do you like to think you would do were you that sales person?

When faced with temptation, isn't it nearly always easier to haggle over price than principle? It's something to think about the next time you find yourself faced with temptation.

Exercise

1. Can a case <u>ever</u> be made for violating copyright laws? If "Yes," what argument can be made?

2. Is anyone harmed when something is copied where there was absolutely no intent from the outset to buy the material?

3. Is violating a copyright ever an act <u>void</u> of theft? Explain.

4. Can a lawful case be made for the use of radar detectors in automobiles? If "Yes," why haven't more than two states outlawed their use? If "No," why are they outlawed in any jurisdiction?

5. Were you to discover a malfunctioning meter failing to record the use of electricity in your home, when would you report it?

6. Has the amount of a mistake made favoring you in a transaction ever been a factor in your calling attention to the error? If "Yes," what is the cutoff and how is it justified?

7.   Have you ever felt pressured to buy something you didn't want by someone you felt was more interested in the sale from his perspective than from yours? If you answered "Yes," how did you respond to such pressure?

CHAPTER THREE

"Testing Right versus Wrong"

Making the right decision when little competition is presented by alternative right answers is relatively easy. It was former President Johnson who often remarked that making the right decision is easy when there is only one right choice. It's where there are <u>more</u> than one right answers that the decisions get tough.

Business decisions arising from applying one's personal ethics are frequently fraught with shades of grey rather than presenting absolute right or wrong alternatives. Of all such examples in modern time, perhaps the best is that which President Harry Truman faced shortly after assuming the presidency in April, 1945, upon the death of President Franklin D. Roosevelt.

Meeting with newly installed President Truman on April 25,1945, then Secretary of War Henry L. Stimpson and General Leslie R. Groves handed Truman a report covering the history of the Manhattan Project insisting he read it immediately. Thus was the former Senator from Missouri thrust into the vanguard of decision making concerning America's atomic power monopoly.

Once the A-Bomb had been tested he was advised to use the deadly device on a military target in Japan. At issue was whether the Japanese should be warned ahead of time or if the bomb should be dropped with no forewarning, followed by a demand for unconditional surrender.

Some of his advisors favored a naval blockade, followed by bringing about a Japanese surrender through conventional bombing. Turning to George C. Marshall, Truman inquired, "What do you think, General? Can we finish them off with a blockade and conventional bombing?"

"It didn't work in Germany," replied Marshall. "We leveled their cities, cut off their supplies, and it still took ground forces to finish the job."

When it was estimated that at a minimum, half-a-million men would be lost on land and sea as a result of such a plan, Truman was appalled.

Meanwhile, one key scientist on the Manhattan Project had become convinced the bomb's use on a Japanese target would be morally wrong. "Would it be more moral to end up with half-a-million American casualties and millions of Japanese dead from conventional bombing?", inquired the President. "Moralists sit in the grandstand," exclaimed Truman on more than one occasion. His was the ethical and moral decision to make.

Prior to making his momentous decision, Harry Truman told Secretary of State James Byrnes,

"Someone even suggested that I warn the Japanese ahead of time exactly where and when we intended to drop the bomb. I said, 'Fine, but what about the pilot who flies the plane? Who'll explain to his family that he was shot down because his [fool] president told the enemy he was coming?'"

Well, the rest is history. Atomic bombs were dropped, not once but twice before the Japanese capitulated and surrendered unconditionally.

Later while talking with President Truman, J. Robert Oppenheimer, the Manhattan Project Director of Operations, complained that he had blood on his hands. Truman's response?

"All you did, Professor was make the bomb. I'm the guy who made the decision to drop it. And if American lives were on the line and I had to make the same decision again, I'd make it [snaps fingers] like that."

As in so many decisions, myriad issues had to be weighed by Truman in reaching a conclusion in this instance. The process is similar in nearly all personal testing of right versus wrong. A clear head, good advice, sound reasoning, and respected role models, are all helpful in deciding an issue.

But in the final analysis, it is the sum of all you have ever been taught, all you have ever experienced, and all decisions you have made in the past, that will exert ultimate influence on your choices, right or wrong.

Exercise

1. Can you recall being faced with more than one right choice though the issue called for but a singular judgment? What influenced you to decide as you did?

2. Can you think of any <u>business</u> decision you have made where there were no shades of grey present beckoning you to consider alternate choices?

3. Do you remember any <u>personal</u> decision made where there were no shades of grey present pulling you in the direction of alternate choices?

4. Analyze each of President Truman's options in deciding whether to use the atomic bomb in the waning days of World War II. Which alternative do you think seemed best then? Which seems best now?

5. How often does the vantage of looking back in retrospect cause you to reassess or second guess a judgment? Are these second guesses realistic in light of <u>all information available</u> when you made your decision originally?

CHAPTER FOUR

"Silence: Golden or Yellow?"

A young woman at lunch time rushed breathlessly into a small town bakery crowded with noon hour patrons. Excitedly she inquired, "Is the birthday cake ready that I ordered for Ruth?"

An older salesclerk went off and returned with a large sheet cake covered with white icing. Customers waiting for their orders to be filled couldn't help but notice the beautifully decorated cake with delicate pink-iced roses surrounding the scripted message, "Your <u>best</u> Birthday yet, Ruth --- May it be <u>worse</u> than all others to come!"

And who was Ruth? Obviously someone thought of highly by her office coworkers who had gone to a lot of trouble to order a cake with such a unique message. Oh, you know the "Ruths" of this world, those people who wherever they are work to make most days a little more pleasant for everyone. Undoubtedly an office party was planned that afternoon for the birthday person, where office coworkers would momentarily revert to boys and girls, regressing to the hoopla and free-spirited fun of birthdays past.

But first the cake --- the main prop of any birthday party --- had to be procured. Informed that the cost was $17.96, the young lady took out her checkbook, wrote a check and handed it to the clerk, who went to the cash register to ring up the sale.

Moments later an obviously irate manager appeared with the young lady's check in hand. "We can't take your check, Miss," she hissed, though loud enough for all in the small shop to hear. "You once gave us a bad check and it is our policy <u>never</u> again to accept a check from someone who has hung bad paper on us."

The young woman's face reddened. Her mouth tightened as she was subjected to a verbal barrage which seemed to last forever. Meanwhile the older clerk stood in the background, in contrast looking markedly sympathetic and compassionate.

"But," protested the young woman, "that returned check was the bank's fault. They had placed my deposit in another's account, as they pointed out in a letter mailed to you. They even sent me a copy," she concluded.

With a surly look of disdain, the shop manager said, "We don't care what happened. Once we get a bad check for <u>any</u> reason, our policy is <u>never again</u>. Why we wouldn't accept a check of yours if you were the Mayor of this town. Cash is the <u>only</u> way we will now deal with you."

Imagine how mortified the young woman felt. She would gladly have vanished from sight had such an option been available. <u>Anything</u> but to stand here singled out for ridicule and disgrace. Her face turned an even deeper crimson, her shoulders sagged, and her spirits plummeted as if she had been physically struck.

Those standing around either stared at the store manager in disbelief or riveted their eyes on the young, embarrassed customer, though it was difficult to assess whether the greater embarrassment was that of the chastised and demoralized young woman or belonged to those who had witnessed her ordeal.

What would you have done had you been standing in the store at that moment? Ignored the incident, only later feeling guilty because you had failed to speak up? Vowed never to shop in that establishment again? Spoken up posthaste in defense of the young lady who was being so obviously mistreated? Or would you have pretended not to have heard what went on, going about your affairs all the while assuring yourself that whatever business at hand was none of yours?

A man standing several customers deep at the counter jostled his way to the front. Speaking haltingly at first, then with great resolve, he inquired, "How --- just how much is the cake?" Informed of the amount by the somewhat startled manager he wrote a check of his own to cover the transaction, accepting the young lady's check in return for his.

As you examine the following exercise,

imagine yourself standing in the small bakery that day. What would you have done?

Exercise

1. Why do you suppose only one person came to the young woman's defense? What caused others to hold back?

2. Of those present, what do you think caused this lone man to respond to someone he didn't even know?

3. Had you been present, how do you think you would have responded?

4. What do you perceive were the managers' needs and what course of action would best respond to her needs?

5. How much influence do others' exert over your ethical responses?

6. List incidents similar to this that have occurred in your own life or in the lives of friends or acquaintances.

7. Rewrite one such incident with emphasis on the most desirable ethical outcome for all involved.

CHAPTER FIVE

"The Gray Market for Airfare Coupons"

Is traveling First Class worth a little deceit? If so, how much deception would you be party to before deciding you were sacrificing too much in exchange for better travel arrangements?

Frequent-flier bonus programs were first introduced by American Airlines in 1981. Ever since airlines have tried in vain to stop coupon brokers from buying bonus awards from legitimate passengers and then selling them to what airlines refer to as illegitimate passengers. A glance at the "Tickets" classified ads in any major newspaper suggests what little success airlines have encountered in this regard.

What is wrong with buying airline tickets from a broker? Says Kansas Deputy Attorney General Art Weiss, "I know of no law, state or local, that makes it illegal to buy tickets from coupon brokers." True enough, but to use a brokered ticket the traveler must often lie, claiming either to be the person who earned it or in some cases a relative or business associate of one who did.

Brokers buy bonus tickets paying about 1.5 cents a mile. Travelers sell them in order to recoup some of their travel expenses, often reasoning that such bonus coupons or tickets are their rightful possession to do with as they please. However, nearly all airlines expressly forbid the transfer of such tickets or coupons, creating what is often referred to as the "gray market of air travel", dealing in an estimated $25 million worth of tickets a year.

A brokered ticket often offers unabashed luxury at fire-sale rates. First-class international tickets bought through brokers can save up to 70 percent off the airline's published price. In turn, business-class seats can frequently be acquired for little more than a coach ticket, while coach coupons go at a price competitive with those sold as advance-purchases.

The problem? Each coupon clearly states it cannot be traded for cash nor is it to be used by a traveler other than the one to whom it was issued. But according to the American Association of Discount Travel Brokers, fewer than one percent of those purchasing brokered tickets are ever caught.

Still, there are risks. Getting caught would require the traveler to surrender his ticket at the check-in counter, buy a full-fare ticket if desiring to travel that day, and possibly receive no compensation from the broker from whom the ticket was purchased. In addition, the airline may seize any remaining frequent-flier points accrued by the passenger who sold the coupon or ticket in the first place.

So though the original transaction between passenger and ticket broker may be legal, obvious deception is part of the process from the outset. As mentioned, in many cases the purchaser of a flight coupon must claim to be a relative of the person who earned it initially. Some brokers encourage purchasers to lie, if necessary, at departure time. Claiming to be related in some manner to the purchaser is described as "no big deal". Underscoring the problem, many classified ads proclaim the need to be "male" or "female", obviously a means of furthering the deception since the specific ticket on hand must be used by the "original" purchaser.

What's the answer? Is the gray market airline coupon practice right? Is it wrong? Or just shady? Could the ultimate issue be one of how "shady" you are willing to be when it comes to dealing with airfare coupons or tickets issued to someone else?

Exercise

1. How much deceit would you be willing to participate in to fly cheaper or to upgrade your flight?

2. Do you think it is wrong to buy brokered airline tickets? Explain.

3. Are bonus tickets or coupons the rightful property of the airline or the original passenger? Can you defend both positions?

4. When trafficking in brokered tickets, is it simply a matter of breaking airline company policy or do you see something inherently wrong in the practice?

5. If you thought you would never be caught, would such belief make a difference in your deciding to purchase and use a brokered ticket?

6. Would you sense any moral responsibility toward one who lost all frequent-flier accrued mileage due to your attempting to fly on his/her frequent-flier pass?

CHAPTER SIX

"Helping the Less Fortunate"

It's almost impossible to avoid the homeless, the hungry, the mentally disturbed, those persons in need found on the streets of every major city. Whether going to or leaving work, enroute to church or heading for a night on the town, the poor, as the Good Book reminds us, are always among us.

The ethical problem? How should we respond? The temptation is to pretend we don't see them; to ignore outstretched hands or to ward off the plea, "Any spare change?" But such isn't always possible, as discovered by Dr. Keith R. Ablow, a senior resident in psychiatry at the New England Medical Center in Boston and described in a special report to the Washington Post.

One night after having just gone to sleep he was awakened while on call at the Boston Veterans Administration Hospital to interview a 56 year-old male who was divorced, homeless and complaining of depression with a history of alcohol dependency.

A newcomer to the emergency room, this street person had recently lost his job, his wife, and finally his home. Having slept in shelters for weeks, this evening he had sobered up too late to get a shelter bed. Alone in the freezing wind, his grief and exhaustion weighed more heavily than ever. He desperately wanted to be admitted to the hospital. At least it was <u>some</u> place to stay for the night.

Denying any symptoms of clinical depression or other major mental illness, including the absence of an inclination to harm himself, the resident had no choice: the hospital was over-flowing with patients that night. There was simply no legitimate reason to admit this person.

So by giving him a few dollars of his own, the doctor sent the man away to spend the night on the subway, leaving the physician "with the nagging guilt that I could, or should, have done more for this man."

In one situation or another we have all been there. The people we pass on the streets scan our faces expectantly, looking for any sign of potential help, wondering if we're friend or foe. As much as we might like to help, we feel overburdened with the onslaught, fearing much as did the young physician in the emergency room, that we will be inundated with similar requests if we take a special interest in any one of them.

Yet, neither are we satisfied when avoiding the stares of the homeless, knowing there is <u>something</u> we could do. But fear plays a dominant role in our refusal to become involved. Perhaps it is the unspoken fear, "There but for the grace of God go

I." Or do we find ourselves disturbed with the thought that people in need might take advantage of us, using our good will and charity for causes we deem unacceptable?

Exploitation aside, sometimes when honest we admit we're fearful of being harmed physically. And though possible, is this sufficient reason to stand aloof, rendering no aid?

One of Thomas Jefferson's favorite biblical stories was that of the Good Samaritan. The good people of the day passed by the injured man in a hurry to get on with their business, perhaps not wanting to soil their clothes. It was the lowly Samaritan, despised by all "respectable" people of his day, who stopped, ministered to the man's injuries, took him to get care, and promised to return to repay the innkeeper for any additional expenses the patient might incur.

In weighing just what it is we do to help the unfortunate of our day, consider: who is the modern Good Samaritan? And finally, for just a moment ask yourself, "Could the world use one more?"

Exercise

1. Write down three examples of ways you have seen people aid the less fortunate. Which of the three are you most likely to apply in your future dealings with those who are down, if not yet out?

2. Had you been the psychiatric resident on call in the Emergency Room at the Boston Veterans Administration Hospital when this street person entered seeking help at 1 A.M., what would have been your response?

3. Do you think the patient was being honest or just naive in denying major psychological symptoms that would have guaranteed immediate hospital admission?

4. What is the best way for you to help those who are downtrodden?

5. What fears prevent you from helping homeless persons encountered on the streets?

6. A trilogy of considerations:

    a. Do you know of any modern day Good Samaritans?

    b. Would you like to be one?

    c. What can you do to become one?

CHAPTER SEVEN

"Acceptable Behavior on Company Time?"

Shortly after the work day had begun the phone rang at Sandra's desk where she was busy compiling data relating to the firm's current priority contract. The caller was her Mother, who was fighting a bout of depression. Again. Mostly Sandra listened to the older woman's despairing uneasiness offering only an occasional comment as her Mother talked through her concerns.

Meanwhile, Sandra's manager dropped by her office where in short order he deduced she was involved in a personal call. He left without comment.

Later that day he returned to her work station reiterating once again company policy regarding personal phone calls either received or made during the work day. Sandra admitted to accepting occasional personal calls at work but was quick to point out that she didn't stop working during such incoming calls, "As," she added testily, "you witnessed when in here this morning." This brief exchange ended with strained feelings as is usually the case when both parties believe they are right.

Was Sandra's position reasonable? Indeed, what is acceptable behavior on company time? Listening to many office workers one would conclude that abuses of all descriptions are rife in work places everywhere.

For instance, if it is understood that office hours are from 9 to 5, there should be little question but that employees are expected to be in place and working by 9 and up until 5. Theoretically sound, isn't it? But what happens in reality?

Some operate with the belief they are to be in the office physically from 9 to 5. Mistakenly, they assume that as long as they are present they are at work. True: they may be at work but they are not necessarily about work.

Visiting with coworkers, discussing current events or comparing notes on pending or past events contributes nothing to the job. And when such behavior occurs within the prescribed work hours, not only is one's employer deprived of a fair return on a single worker's contribution but a similar investment is lost when other workers are distracted from their jobs due to the affect of such socializing on company time.

Though some business leaders are of the opinion that they are unable to change values and morals of employees, a common consensus holds that behavior of employees on the job can be changed. Whatever approach is chosen to affect acceptable behavior in the work place, the most important consideration is what type of ethics program top management is willing to support by word <u>and</u> deed. For in determining what is acceptable on company time, employees will look up, not down. Top management leads by example. Nowhere is the old adage, "monkey see - monkey do" more applicable.

Where firms have instituted flex-time, allowing workers to begin and end their work days at varying hours, supervisors have complained that some employees arrive at the later but leave at the earlier hour. An eight hour work day is thus often reduced to six or fewer hours.

Another work-related ethical issue arises when an employee leaves his or her employment with a given company with the unresolved question, "How much of what I created on the job can I take with me?" Or, "Is it appropriate to leave a hard copy of systems I instituted while working there, taking with me the disc on which they are stored?"

This problem most often involves work relating to intangibles such as computer systems designed for a certain company. In separating what belongs to the firm from what the individual can rightfully claim as personal property, the debate frequently focuses on the issue of creativity.

Did the firm hire you to contribute what you could creatively to problem solving? Was there an understanding at the outset as to what would belong to the firm and that to which the individual could lay personal claim?

Where no such agreement exists, is the company right in insisting that all performed work that relates to the job description belongs to the firm? If the issue were building plans and the employee executed these drawings while working for an architectural firm, there would seem little question as to the firm's rightful ownership of the plans. Following similar logic, an invention resulting from work directly involving company time would belong to the corporation, not the individual --- that is <u>unless</u> a prior agreement had been reached stipulating otherwise.

Company time is precisely that --- company time. If so, should workers paid for their contributions and efforts expect ownership rights to what was performed on company time?

Exercise

1. What do you feel is acceptable office etiquette regarding personal phone calls on the job?

2. Under what conditions is flex-time most likely to work well?

3. Can you imagine circumstances where flex-time would create more problems than it would solve? Explain.

4. How much rightful claim does a firm have regarding an employee's output?

5. Cite instances where an employee would seemingly have a legitimate claim to work related contributions upon leaving the company.

6. How many exceptions to these instances can you cite. Under what circumstances would they most likely arise?

CHAPTER EIGHT

"Something for Nothing?"

Does it sometimes seem the whole world is looking for something for nothing? An employee in a legal firm was recently charged with returning to the scene where one of the firms' clients had fallen, enlarging the sidewalk hole with a pick-axe before photographing the site as a potential courtroom exhibit.

Insurance companies offer a litany of examples of unethical claims. People have been known to stage car wrecks to get insurance carriers to cover damages incurred elsewhere. So common was homeowner insurance fraud in one town that after taking out sizable protection on his home, the newly insured inquired of his agent: "How much would I get if this place burned down tonight?" Responded the agent wryly, "Oh, I'd say about ten years."

But fraud is hardly a laughing matter, particularly when its cost must of necessity be passed on to the general public, meaning you and me. Not long ago a baggage handler in a busy airport complained about people who make false claims of contents in a suitcase lost while in transit by the airline.

When asked to list lost items, he said people enumerate all kinds of things, including expensive jewelry, top-of-the-line cameras, designer labeled clothes and even furs. "Inevitably," he stated, "when the bag is recovered it contains old clothes, maybe a running suit and a pair of sneakers with no tread."

Years ago a businessman spoke to a group of youth on the theme, "Does the World Owe Me a Living?" His conclusion was that the world owes <u>no one</u> a living; that the world's only responsibility is to provide a climate where a living can be earned.

Yet, if making and filing false claims is any indication, there are those who feel that all is fair in love, war, and the pursuit of their own individual well-being. Perhaps the likelihood of this pursuit of something for nothing increases in direct proportion to the prospect of getting caught.

If this is so, it may mean that many times we choose to do the right thing for the wrong reasons. Rather than pursuing a course of action because it is right, we are more likely to choose a response based on whether or not we think we can get away with it.

A keen observer of human nature notes, "A sleeping pill is a poor substitute for a guilty conscience." And while this is true, it is equally correct to conclude that rationalization offers scant comfort in overcoming action you know is wrong. For make no mistake: to attempt to get something for nothing is to receive something at another's expense. Ultimately the piper will be paid, whether the piper is the individual shopper who pays more because we didn't pay our fair share or the company's profit and loss column resulting in our gain and their loss. Of course there is no doubt but that such losses will be passed on to consumers in one form or another.

Some conclude that one's true character emerges when a person thinks something can be had for nothing. Greed takes over, with individuals going to almost any lengths to achieve a desired end.

Fortunately, most people recognize the folly in seeking something for nothing, being willing to pay a fair price in exchange for an equitable return. Ultimately it is a tradeoff, a question of how much you are willing to give, give up or demand of yourself to achieve a specific aim.

All of which reminds us of the late H. L. Hunt's response when someone asked him how he had acquired so much during his lifetime. He replied by enunciating a simple formula consisting of but three steps. "First, decide what it is that you want. Second, determine what you are willing to give up to get it, and third, get on with the task."

The next time you feel tempted to dream about winning the lottery, coming into a sizable inheritance, or investing in that single stock issue that will set you up for life, recall Mr. Hunt's sage advice, realizing that truly, there is no free lunch.

And now, on with those essential tasks necessary to bringing you whatever you most desire from life.

Exercise

1. Other than the appeal of it being easy, what are other lures of getting something for nothing?

2. What arguments do some people make when claiming, "The world owes me a living?" Is there any credence to such arguments?

3. Do you think a person's true character emerges when an individual thinks something can be had for nothing? Cite two instances where you have seen this happen.

4.   How conscious are you of the tradeoffs required to achieve most any goal or end in your life?

5.   Do you think of tradeoffs as applying more to material or non-material (health, happiness, etc.) gain?

CHAPTER NINE

"Taking Pride in the One You Have Become"

Whenever a company's reputation begins to erode it is difficult for leaders to reverse the tide, much less to change public opinion. Similarly, when people decide a person lacks integrity, it is difficult for them to alter their perceived images.

Obviously the best approach is to take continual soundings of your own evolving ethical base, asking yourself the pointed question: "Do I want to live in the kind of world where everyone acts like me?"

Though there is apparent ethical virtue in always being "totally honest," such practice may in fact be anything but. Those who insist on telling the whole truth at all times and under all circumstances may be responding with a mix of crudity and cruelty, for often rather than telling the truth for its own sake, their goal is to strike out and hurt another.

Still, we find it refreshing to observe honest candor, especially when discovered in the least likely places.

So it was in the political arena --- where

many view ethics from a somewhat jaded perspective, at best --- that in 1962 Kevin Coleman, then Mayor of Woonsocket, Rhode Island, made a bid for governor. In an important primary speech he said, "I'll be frank about it. I'm a candidate for the personal opportunity as far as Kevin Coleman is concerned. Personal prestige and position is [sic] the reason why any candidate runs. This seeking of the position solely for fighting for the people is a lot of hogwash."

No, candidate Coleman did not prevail in the primary and while voters may have appreciated his honesty too much for his own good, in any event here was that rare candidate who admittedly put his own interests first. While honest with the electorate, was he ethical? Could such a philosophy cause one to feel good about himself at the end of a day or at the close of a career?

In contrast stands 39-year-old Fred Gibbons, CEO and co-founder of Software Publishing Corporation, who believes that today you need to provide a coherent, carefully developed, and clearly explained set of values to capture employee loyalty and to build a team spirit that thrives. These "rules of the game" as he calls them, permeate every aspect of his operations: and everyone must live by the code, especially the boss.

Reports analyst Rich Sherlund of Goldman, Sachs & Co., "Fred [Gibbons] is the most honest, straightforward CEO I know."

One can imagine that living with himself is

not the most difficult task Fred Gibbons confronts. Similar pride can be taken by others in all walks of life who choose to live ethically.

Lt. Col. David Hackworth, once described by General Creighton Abrams as, "the best battalion commander I ever saw in the United States Army," predicted as early as 1970 that the Viet Cong would occupy Saigon by 1975. Not only was the war going bad politically, but Hackworth strongly felt we were losing the war on the battlefield, with bad tactics, limp leadership and poorly trained, dispirited troops. Finally, in 1971, Colonel Hackworth spoke before a national television audience on "Issues and Answers", claiming that the body counts and "razzle-dazzle" briefings were lies, and that the generals didn't know how to fight a guerrilla war. Not unexpectedly, Hackworth's revealed integrity was not appreciated within the service. Eventually he resigned. Whatever else can be said, he had not fallen victim to the trap of "to get along, go along" --- especially when he could not do so in good conscience.

Getting along by going along when you know, or strongly suspect the course of action is wrong, will not help you take pride in the one you are becoming. Rather, it is by remaining true to your own high ideals and the best you have instilled in your own character development that will lead you to conclude, "Yes, I would like to live in the kind of world we'd have if everyone lived their lives following a code of ethics similar to mine."

By working at all times to bring out your best and at least doing nothing to hinder your better self from acting, you can take pride in the one you have become and in the one you are continuing to become. For truly, school is never out for one seeking to rise to the best ethical options existent in a given situation.

Exercise

1. Describe the kind of world that would exist if all others had ethical codes similar to yours.

2. Have you ever been subjected to or known those who have been victims of someone purporting to be "perfectly honest"? What do you feel are the real motives of such a person?

3. What causes a political figure such as Mayor Coleman to be so blatantly honest?

4. Though perhaps admired for his honesty, what did the Mayor's stated views suggest about his ethics?

5. What are the more important benefits in being known as a straightforward CEO? Is such a posture likely to affect an individual differently at home than at work? Why?

6. What do you need to do differently in your daily life to afford you an even greater sense of ethical pride in the one you are becoming?

7. List those people you can enlist to help you achieve a goal of practicing more lofty ethics or at a minimum help you maintain your ethical momentum.

CHAPTER TEN

"New Plateaus of Individual Integrity"

In spite of an abundance of stories to the contrary, evidence exists that the tide is turning in favor of ethical conduct, both among individuals, corporations, and within government agencies. Surely this is a force to be reckoned with as we broach the threshold of the last decade of this century.

But whatever improvement in our collective ethic, it starts with the individual. Being true to yourself, as the Bard of Avon reminded us, is where integrity begins. Not so much an <u>external</u> force, but a vital <u>internal</u> one is at play here.

For instance: what would you do if you felt strongly about an idea but your superiors were threatened by your position? Would it be more ethical for you to (1) suppress your thoughts; (2) continue with the "old" way of doing things even though you KNEW your plan would save your employer money, or (3) direct your energies tactfully toward instituting your idea?

Though impossible to determine the

tactfulness of Clarence Saunders, a clerk in a "mom and pop" grocery store in Memphis, he did suggest to his boss that customers should be allowed to select their own groceries from the shelves just as they selected food from the then-new cafeteria-style restaurants.

Fired for wasting time on "foolish ideas," Saunders spent four years raising enough capital to open what became the successful Piggly-Wiggly grocery chain. This bold idea of his gave impetus to the establishment of the modern supermarket concept. It also made Saunders a wealthy man, all resulting from his actions as an ethical employee who shared with his employer an idea --- though unpopular --- he thought would help achieve the goal of increased sales.

Business ethics, though formerly ignored, has in the last 15 years achieved curriculum status in most business schools. Prior to 1978 one searched almost in vain for a textbook on business ethics. Today a choice may be made from among dozens.

And on the personal front, there seems to be a renewed appreciation of what the philosopher, Kant, had in mind when he wrote, "Truthfulness in statements which cannot be avoided is the formal duty of an individual to everyone, however great may be the disadvantage accruing to himself or to another." For others to be able to accept your words as absolute truth as you understand it, will free you from enslavement of uncertainty and low self-esteem, both embodied in the conscious thought of one who feels the mistrust of others whenever offering his opinions.

Yet, it was Thomas Jefferson who argued, "A strict observance of the written laws is doubtless one of the high duties of a good citizen, but it is not the highest. Of a higher obligation," he maintained, "were the laws of necessity, self preservation, and saving our country when in danger."

Almost two centuries later Winston Churchill seemed to agree that good men do and should deceive in pursuit of noble causes. Churchill withheld information from Parliament and Franklin D. Roosevelt about Enigma --- the decoding machine the Poles stole from the Germans --- giving the Allies access to German secrets during World War II.

As D-Day approached, the Allies deceived Hitler, persuading him that a landing would take place near Calais and not on the Normandy beaches. And what was the consequence? The saving of thousands of allied lives and perhaps the invasion. In defending such decisions, Churchill said the truth is sometimes so important it has to be protected by a "bodyguard of lies." Obviously the means were used to justify the ends.

But do the means <u>always</u> justify the end? In a speech regarding America's future, Peter M. Dawkins asserts he has no doubt we can be the best. He notes, "We can be the leader. We can go on from where we are today to build a society whose <u>freedom</u> and <u>dignity</u> and <u>confidence</u> and <u>justice</u> and <u>humanity</u>

--- for all our people --- exceeds anything ever seen on this planet. We have it within our power to do these things."

"But, for us to do so," he continues, "we must recapture our traditional commitment to those standards of integrity and trust which, throughout our history, have been the foundation of our greatness." In conclusion Dawkins says, "It seems to me that then, and only then, will the future our children inherit be a bright one, a future that remains solid and strong, and reflects in a practical and realistic way, our hopes and our dreams."

Excellence in individuals, as is the case with corporations, will not be derived from perfection but from a willingness to recognize and honestly attempt to address imperfections. Thus, tomorrow's leaders will be those who recognize that acceptable customs of the past, i.e., dumping pollutants into rivers, cannot be supported in the present. Ethical choices then, once and for all, will be seen as good business, dismantling the argument that "business ethics" is an oxymoron. It isn't. If anything, good business is good ethics, as will be revealed even more clearly in the 21st century, where an abundance of new opportunities at elevated plateaus awaits individuals of solid integrity.

Exercise

1. What evidence have you observed in the last decade of improvement in ethical conduct for (a) individuals, (b) corporations, and (c) government agencies?

2. How would you respond concerning a moral issue about which your immediate superior's feelings run counter to your own?

3. Describe an idea that you failed to share regarding improving a product or situation due to personal concerns as to how your suggestion would be received.

4. Can you think of an example where responding ethically paid off materially for one who chose to stand up and speak out, even though the position being defended was unpopular?

5. What exceptions can you think of to Kant's assertion, "Truthfulness in statements which cannot be avoided is the formal duty of an individual to everyone, however great may be the disadvantage accruing to himself or to another"?

6. What role can you play in helping America recapture its traditional commitment to high standards of integrity and trust?

7. Can you think of customs that were acceptable throughout our culture in the past but would not pass ethical scrutiny today?

PART II.

Applying Ethics

INTERPERSONALLY

PART II.

"Applying Ethics

INTERPERSONALLY"

Dr. Fred B. Craddock of Emory University's Candler School of Theology maintains that what is needed for ethics to improve is practice --- just plain practice. Yet if anything, it appears that when applying ethics interpersonally, many practice but what they practice are their skills at <u>ethics inaction</u> rather than <u>ethics in action</u>.

Several examples can be cited to support

such an assertion. Rather than loving people and using things, we are prone to use people and love things, as Alexander Pope warned us against doing.

For instance, we know that AIDS cases are increasing in nearly all areas of the world. One of the most perplexing problems is encountered when health professionals contract the deadly disease. What is their responsibility to their patients? Is it ethical for such professionals to assume that they can take measures to assure their patients don't become infected or should they tell patients up front of their diagnoses and the precautions they will be taking to protect those who have entrusted their health to them?

Many dentists and physicians complain that once their patients learn the practioner is infected with the HIV-virus that causes AIDS, there will be no need to inform them of any planned precautions for these people will no longer be patients. At least not theirs. While conceding this is probable, is this reason for concluding patients should not be informed?

Ethics inaction or ethics in action? Which will it be?

Juries in several states are currently struggling with the aftermath of AIDS infected health professionals whose patients have become contaminated during the course of treatment. In many instances the physician or dentist is now dead, with legal proceedings ensnaring estates of the deceased.

The spill-over from personal, to interpersonal, to business ethics is nowhere more clearly observed than in some of these cases. First comes the personal ethical decision by the individual practitioner to withhold information regarding the infection. The next stage is how the practitioner proceeds interpersonally in treating each patient after the HIV-virus causing AIDS been diagnosed. Finally, when a medical facility in which the physician or dentist practices or has practiced takes no action in attempting to inform former or current patients of the problem then we can conclude ethical lapses have occurred in all three areas, i.e., (1) personally, (2) interpersonally, and (3) institutionally.

Though some AIDS experts claim these decisions violate neither laws nor any clear ethical standards, the quandary faced --- especially by those exposed to the risk of contracting AIDS without their knowledge --- becomes apparent, if to none other than these exposed patients and their loved ones. Juries in several states have already begun rendering verdicts on what ethical standards should be applied in such cases. Not surprisingly, juries tend to favor patients, not infected health practitioners.

Or what can be said for ethical action applied interpersonally when people who could intervene stand by, doing nothing? No, this isn't a situation of physical abuse but, rather, of verbal abuse designed to torment another.

At Maryland's St. Mary's College, the first woman to play college baseball quit the team alleging sexism among her teammates, coach, and athletic director.   She cited instances of teammates reading aloud a degrading article from <u>Penthouse</u> magazine during a team bus ride, male players lewdly describing pornographic videos scheduled to be shown at a planned party, and speaking obscenely of female genitalia.   <u>USA Today</u> reported her former coach as saying, "It was just guys being guys."

But is "guys being guys" an euphemism for avoiding the issue of confronting interpersonal ethics or lack of same, i.e., <u>ethics inaction</u>?

Using another person is unethical, regardless of the manner of use, when the other party benefits in no discernible way. Not surprisingly, fathers of daughters become some of the most vocal champions railing out against verbal abuse when it is <u>their</u> offspring who are victimized. But must personal ties to the victim be a prerequisite of coming to the defense of one subjected to such abuse?

Much ethical inaction between the sexes centers on sexual abuse. Often, but not always, this abuse is physical. Marilyn Van Derbur Atler, Miss America in 1958, has gone public with the revelation that her millionaire father sexually assaulted her for 13 years. Her father, who is now deceased, reportedly victimized her from the time she was 5 until she reached age 18.

Laboring under a tyranny of terror as a child, she never told anyone. When as an adult she finally told her mother, her mother responded by looking at her matter-of-factly and saying, "I don't believe you. It's in your fantasy." Said Van Derbur Atler, "I felt like I'd been kicked in the stomach."

So much for wondering why more children don't report acts of sexual assault to their parents or to other trusted adults.

Others who have been sexually molested remain quiet out of fear and shame. That they won't talk is the most lethal weapon in an abuser's arsenal. Exist there better examples of interpersonal ethics inaction? One would be hard pressed to describe any.

Rape, and date rape specifically, are other noxious examples of ethics inaction between two parties. College campuses are only now becoming aware of this growing problem that needs to be redressed. In all too many instances it won't be a pursuit of <u>The Right Thing</u> per se that stems the tide but rather an institutional fear of legal reprisal that will redress this problem. But however addressed, this is <u>The Right Thing</u>, isn't it? Still, we are left to wonder if this is but another case of arriving at the right solution but for the wrong reason.

If applying ethics interpersonally seems to reach one of its lowest ebbs in relations between the sexes, much of the fault can be attributed to skepticism toward rape victims in courtrooms, effectively discouraging women from reporting sex crimes. Notes Gill Freeman, a Miami lawyer who chairs the Florida Supreme Court Gender Bias Study Implementation Commission, "There is still in Florida a widespread belief that people who are sexually molested, raped or assaulted somehow precipitate that action.

"Unfortunately, evidence of this attitude has been found to exist among law enforcement personnel, jurors and judges in the state of Florida," she concludes.

Further proof of such ethical insensitivity is observed in the South Florida case where police officers and court personnel asked a victim whether she had **enjoyed** [italics supplied] the rape. In an equally appalling instance, a sitting judge advised a convicted rapist, "You have to take them out to dinner first like the rest of us."

Chairman Joseph Biden (Democrat) of the Senate Judiciary Committee is championing a federal reform bill that would apply civil rights laws toward addressing this malady. Similar legislation has been proposed from the other side of the senate aisle by Senator Robert Dole (Republican).

Ethical lapses often center around money, especially big sums of money. The day after the state of South Dakota had a lottery drawing for $12.5 million dollars, a convenience clerk found a discarded ticket on the floor behind the counter matching all the right numbers. She paid for, signed, and presented it. Declared the jackpot winner, her "win" was contested by a second clerk, as well as by the store's owners, for the discarded ticket had been issued by the second clerk to a customer who didn't want the $5 ticket, but who wanted five $1 tickets instead. When the customer refused to pay for the ticket, it was left behind the counter where it had been tossed on the floor and subsequently "discovered" by the first clerk.

The store owners sued, claiming that the ticket belongs to them because Lotto America requires store owners to pay for misprints. The second clerk entered the fray claiming it was her responsibility to pay for the ticket since it was she who had made the mistake.

So far readers may wonder where the clear, ethical implication is to be found. As is true in many cases, ethical issues are not as clearcut as we might like to think. However, in this instance the clerk who found the ticket first claimed to have bought the ticket before the drawing. Later, after changing her story, she still disputed she had done anything illegal because the ticket was issued before the drawing and in any event had not been paid for by anyone else.

Legal ramifications of this ethical dilemma are left for authorities in that jurisdiction to decide. Meanwhile, what do you consider the ethical implications? If debating, would you choose to argue the ethical pros or cons in this instance?

As seen in Part I, greed plays a role when ethics are applied personally. It can also prove a major factor when ethics are applied interpersonally.

Telephone marketers selling junk billed as medical equipment to Medicare beneficiaries at wildly inflated prices are just such an example. In one instance a two-inch thick, mattress-size piece of corrugated pink foam was advertised as preventing bedsores.   The cost to suppliers was $28.57.   The product in turn was sold to older Americans for prices ranging as high as $1,132, with the federal government, thanks to Medicare, paying $943 of the cost. Presumably the patient paid the remainder.

Unscrupulous marketers prey on older people, discovering their ailments and convincing them that a particular piece of equipment will bring relief. Other examples of dubious worth sold to the aged include a shoebox-size "paraffin wax bath" billed as relieving arthritic pain. A side effect is that the wax has been known to reach temperatures of 140 degrees, resulting in severe burns to patients. Here the item was purchased for $94.95 by the supplier, yet rented to patients for 15 months for as much as $648!

But yet another example of ethics inaction where one party preys on another is noted in the "flotation pad" ad, a two-inch-thick, 18-inch square of beige foam designed for a wheelchair. Its cost?   A mere $274.

Perhaps the pinnacle of ethics applied interpersonally is found in on-going relationships between two people. Martin Luther once wrote, "There is no more lovely, friendly and charming relationship, communion or company than a good marriage."   And while those enjoying or who have enjoyed the fruits of a good marriage can attest to this, the other side of the coin is that though there is nothing better than a good marriage, there are few things worse than a bad one.

No code of ethics can eliminate pain in relationships, even when evidence exists that ethical misconduct causes many problems for partners. Trust and intimacy require more than candor. One should not keep major secrets nor conceal anything believed important from one's partner in a relationship. And though difficult to determine when such troublesome information should be "volunteered", can't an undisclosed truth be a lie? Still, if there is substantial risk that the other party will feel betrayed or hurt by such revelations, what tradeoff does the obligation of candor raise?

Dr. Frank Pittman, who wrote <u>Private Lies: Infidelity and the Betrayal of Intimacy</u>, says, "It takes very little misinformation to disorient and destroy a relationship. I often point out to people that if I gave them detailed instructions on how to go from Atlanta to New York City, and I threw in only one left turn that was a lie, they would end up in Oklahoma."

If intimacy is the goal in healthy relationships, and surely most individuals in a union place intimacy high on any such list (if not at the top), then dishonesty and secrets must be recognized for what they are: the arch enemies of intimacy.

Once again, the ethical argument focuses on use. People should never be used merely as means for personal gains or as assists in reaching personal goals. Yet, it is obvious that we use others to listen to our tales of woe, to comfort us, to befriend us, or to lift us up when our spirits are down. In this sense ethical issues hardly surface automatically, provided we play similar roles for others, even though not necessarily for the same individual who provided for us in this manner.

When thinking of ethics in action interpersonally, concepts of fairness, caring, and respect for another's needs as well as our own come into play. Treating another as we want to be treated is where the true application of applying ethics interpersonally both begins and ends. Where can such relationships be better studied than in marriage, where individuals are more deeply involved interpersonally because of the very essence of the presence of intimacy? Even so, "open marriage" as espoused nearly two decades ago suggesting that somehow such marriages were the more sophisticated, was an erroneous concept. The implication that couples not accepting one another's philandering were somehow not as mature as were proponents of sexual freedom represented a clear ethical <u>delusion</u> in the name of attempting to foster an ethical <u>illusion</u>.

Fortunately such recreational treatment of sex has given way to recognizing the depth of emotional investment in the sex act. The old argument that being open about "purely sexual" relationships would keep partners from being hurt was naive at best, callous, and of course unethical, at worst.

Ethics professor, Dr. William F. May, labels such persons "emotional prudes", for assuming that "sincerity and honesty provide a kind of solvent that breaks down chemically any and all inconvenient and messy feelings: You hope for the future? But I never promised you a future. Why complain? I am emotionally clean, drip-dry. Why not you?"

To best summarize a discussion of ethics inaction in interpersonal relationships we can do no better than turn to Dr. Rollo May, who writes in <u>Freedom and Destiny</u>, "...the people who can best function in a system of sex without intimacy are those who have little capacity for feeling in the first place."

Compassionate consideration is needed to deal with one another ethically at the interpersonal level, putting another's wants and needs on a par with one's own. Case studies 11 through 20 are designed to help improve skills at responding ethically in interpersonal settings, especially in those one-on-one relationships that account for so much of life's intensity.

CHAPTER ELEVEN

"Whatever Happened to Integrity and Morality?"

To lie, to cheat or to steal, are hardly attributes one wants to embrace. However, a recent ad extolling a community's virtue invited guests to come, <u>steal</u> away for a weekend, <u>cheating</u> boredom and sameness by spending a couple of days doing something different, while at night <u>lying</u> in places frequented by famous past Americans.

Making a virtue out of a liability is occasionally what marketing is all about, I suppose. But problems arise when what is right and moral is viewed as simply another option to ply when attempting to gain the confidence of individuals.

Two of the biggest offenders in this regard seem to be time-share resorts and membership campgrounds. Prospects are informed they have won a major prize, usually a car, only to be told after arriving on site that instead they are to receive a consolation prize.

In one instance the prize was a television projection system. When the hapless prey asked for his prize, he was informed they are not kept on the property because of storage problems, but shipment was promised, providing an $89.95 shipping and handling charge was paid up front. For this the "winner" received something akin to a large piece of plywood and a magnifying glass to be set in front of the television set.

Another ploy is the proffered gem stone collection, reportedly worth more than a thousand dollars. The true retail price is often substantially less, of course.

A motorized boat was offered by one company. Believe it or not, the "winner" received an inflatable rubber raft and a hand-held electric beater!

Free prizes and vacations held out as "bait" to those who will view a property offering represent a relatively new concept in marketing. Says Tom Gallagher, president of the central Virginia office of the Better Business Bureau, "You don't get something for nothing."

Obviously the potential buyer has the right to say, "No," but often pressure is applied, causing many prospects to feel obligated to buy something they really don't want.

For most of us it is not difficult to see the lapse of integrity and morality in such hard-ball selling. But what about the integrity and morality lapse on the part of the purchaser who goes to view such an offering with no intention of buying? When the only reason for viewing an offer is to receive the free prize, isn't this an indication that both the potential seller <u>and</u> the potential purchaser are attempting to take advantage of their counterparts in transactions one is determined to conclude, which at the same time the other is equally determined to avoid?

If so, isn't the lapse of integrity and morality shared equally by both seller and buyer?

Exercise

1. List examples where you feel marketing techniques are blatant abuses in their appeal to what is right and moral. What should and/or can be done about this?

2. Why do you think so many people become victims of what is so obviously a sham from start to finish?

3. What pressures does the buyer feel to make a purchase once a free gift has been bestowed by the seller?

4. Which is the greater lapse of integrity: where the seller doesn't intend to award the proffered gift or where the prospect --- from the outset --- doesn't intend to purchase it?

5. What examples of advertising can you point to that underscore integrity and morality in their appeals?

6. Conversely, what examples of advertising can you point to denoting the decline of integrity and morality?

CHAPTER TWELVE

"How Much Openness In a Relationship?"

Is openness --- a policy of <u>absolute</u> openness --- best in all relationships?

He and she were each in their mid-thirties, neither having previously married. Upon becoming engaged, he proposed an evening where they would share everything from their pasts. At first she thought such openness was a great idea. "After all, why have any secrets from one another?," she reasoned.

On the scheduled evening it was obvious he was becoming more agitated as their talk-fest progressed. Apparently he could not handle detailed knowledge of her past. A few weeks later the engagement was broken and she was left with the haunting question, "Was I too open?"

Can individuals be <u>too</u> open with their partners? Openness and honesty are not one and the same. Couples can be open in agreeing to leave their pasts alone, building a life together on what each has to offer the other in the present. Further, even in the pursuit of honest openness, it is not necessary to tell another <u>everything</u> you know. In fact it can be argued that being <u>too</u> open can do more harm than good.

Certainly such is the situation when your opinion is solicited regarding a matter where your views run counter to those held by another. In fact, sometimes unabashed openness can be cruel, such as persons wanting to make certain you know details ad infinitum of how you have been wronged or taken advantage of by another.

Similarly, sometimes honesty is confused with confession in relationships. Where is it suggested that one should tell <u>all</u> he or she knows? True, sometimes confession can be good for the soul as Saint Augustine reminded us. Generally, though, confession is best made before an objective outsider, preferably someone trained in counseling. Hardly ever is it advisable to engage in confession with one who is subjectively involved in your life.

Of primary consideration regarding openness is (1) the presumed good any such knowledge imparted will bring another and (2) the need to know. Sometimes the need to <u>tell</u> rather than the need to <u>know</u> is paramount. Such openness can then be described as a positive outlet for the one confessing, but a negative experience (if not a curse) for the one hearing the confession.

When considering how much openness is desired in a relationship, couples would do well to examine several possibilities, including: "Is it going to enable him to become a better husband or her a better wife?"   "Will it result in a mate being more appreciative of a spouse?" "Will it enhance the other party's feelings of self-worth?"   Conversely, is it possible that the spouse's guilt feelings will be exacerbated beyond what can be readily borne?

Sometimes partners feel so much pent-up anxiety that they unload all their anxieties on their mates.   After confessing, they proclaim they feel so much better, have such clear consciences, and at last can sleep with ease.   The problem?   Previous symptoms have now been transferred to one's partner with little good having come from such openness. Rather, the end result has simply shifted the burden of guilt from one spouse to another, hardly creating measurable benefits from this newly presumed relationship openness.

Putting the past behind but determining that openness will apply to everything within a relationship from now on may position a marriage so that it can be strengthened beyond anything previously known. The ethical key in applying openness within relationships is to keep it current; don't apply it retroactively. There is simply too much to be lost and too little to be gained.

Exercise

1. What would constitute too much openness in a relationship for you?

2. Why do you think some individuals have so much difficulty handling openness?

3. How do you define the difference between openness and honesty? Is there a difference in your relationship?

4. What three persons or sources would you turn to if you felt the need to confess?

5. Operating under the guise of the "need to know" principle, what would you withhold from a spouse you were trying to spare?

6. Have you ever experienced openness where the burden of guilt simply shifted from another to you?

7. Can you recall instances where you unloaded your guilt or concerns on another, transferring your guilt to them?

CHAPTER THIRTEEN

"Whose is the Test-tube Baby?"

Parenting: a time-honored role most young couples eagerly anticipate if not when planning to marry, then early in the marriage. However, it doesn't always work as hoped.

When one such couple began attempting to conceive they discovered complications. After gynecological tests were conducted it was determined the problem was with the female's uterus, making it impossible for an embryo to attach itself to the uterine wall.

Considering and weighing several alternatives, they decided to try what has commonly been called the "test tube" route. One method involves extracting eggs from the wife's ovaries, then fertilizing them with the husband's sperm. All this is done within the laboratory. Often these fertilized eggs are placed in the wife's uterus, where hopefully a normal pregnancy will occur.

Sometimes multiple births result from this procedure, when more than one implanted fertilized egg is carried full-term, resulting in fraternal twins. But as previously observed, alas, things don't <u>always</u> work as anticipated.

In this instance the couple entered into a contract with another woman wherein she was to serve as a surrogate mother. The couple paid her $10,000 to carry in her womb the embryo resulting from the egg and sperm of the couple having been united in the laboratory, since the wife was unable to accommodate the embryo full term.

Upon giving birth, the surrogate mother sued the couple demanding custody of the child. Though she had no genetic link to the infant she felt her emotional bonds outweighed the biological claim of the parents, rasing the grave question: "What constitutes parenthood?" On the one hand, the biological parents are the genetic parents. Without their having contributed the sperm and egg there would be no child.

Conversely, the surrogate mother argues she, too, has biological ties to the infant. "After all," she stated, "the baby grew in me, used my cells, my blood, and benefitted from the care I took of myself throughout the nine months. I have as much a biological claim as do they."

But does she? If you were the judge, who would be awarded custody?

The couple maintains that they remained emotionally involved with both the surrogate mother and the developing fetus throughout the pregnancy. "If emotional involvement is considered," says the wife, "we were as emotionally involved as possible, our spirits rising and falling with each report from the woman carrying our child."

The surrogate mother counters that she became emotionally attached to the fetus at three months. After giving birth she insisted on a form of joint custody where she could influence the child's upbringing and be awarded regular visitation rights.

Presently there is no known legislation impinging on such matters at either the federal or state levels. As is so often the case, medical technology has outstripped the legislative pace leaving a void that for the moment can only be answered by the judiciary.

Yet the time to play catchup is fast approaching. Still, until legislatures pass laws regarding in vitro (test tube) births, these decisions will be made by the courts. Meanwhile, who do you think has the more legitimate claim: the genetic parents or the surrogate mother?

Exercise

1. What do you consider to be the morality issues centering on test tube fertilization?

2. How much of a genetic claim do you feel a surrogate mother has after carrying a couple's embryo to term?

3. How much credence should be placed on the emotional bonds a surrogate mother feels for a child she carried to term?

4. What constitutes the more important parenting roles: providing the genetic background or carrying a fetus for nearly nine months?

5. Were you to engage the services of a surrogate mother, how would you maintain emotional bonds through a full-term pregnancy?

6. What law or laws do you think would be most just, considering the well being of <u>all</u> parties where surrogate parenting is concerned?

CHAPTER FOURTEEN

"The Right to End Life Stops Where?"

A parent has been diagnosed as suffering from Alzheimer's disease. The condition has been painfully apparent to family members for sometime. Unable to talk or feed herself, and long-since having foregone any sign of recognizing relatives so lovingly embraced in the past, her adult children fear such fate may await one or more of them. Two have entered a pact to assist one another in committing suicide should they ever become convinced such a fate awaits them.

How well does such a decision fit with our professed belief in the sanctity of life? Indeed, where does the right to end life stop?

Taking one's own life in the face of grave illness is hardly anything new. Currently carried on the New York Times best seller list is Derek Humphrey's, Final Exit, a suicide manual offering practical advice for those wanting to escape physical pain and suffering. It is distributed in partnership with the Hemlock Society, an organization existing at least in part to assist people who are convinced death is preferable to life. Meanwhile the country is still reeling from the debate over pathologist, Dr. Jack Kevorkian and what has been dubbed his "suicide machine".

A 54-year-old woman, Janet Adkins of Portland, Oregon, was diagnosed with Alzheimer's disease. She and her husband contacted Dr. Kevorkian of Royal Oak, Michigan, a retired pathologist. Flying to Michigan, the Adkins met with Dr. Kevorkian where they discussed her situation over dinner. Said the physician, "She really wanted to end her life. She was really terrified of what was coming. She had a clear grasp of what she was doing...."

The following Monday Janet Adkins was connected to an intravenous solution containing the drugs thiopental, which induces coma, and potassium chloride, which stops the heart. Several people watched as she pressed a button that administered the lethal chemicals, inducing unconsciousness within seconds and death within minutes. This is the same lethal injection administered criminals on death row, though of course in this instance the decision to die was the patient's.

Under Michigan law, the device itself was not illegal. Michigan also had no jurisdictional law specifically prohibiting physician-assisted suicide. However, when the device was first unveiled, the local Michigan prosecutor's office said that under some circumstances it might attempt to prosecute someone who made the device available as a suicide assist.

That state's legislature has since taken steps to outlaw suicide assists.

The American Medical Association's Code of Ethics permits doctors to forego, stop or withdraw treatment of terminally ill patients but it does not permit doctors to actively assist in ending life.

Back to the late Janet Adkins. Supporting the decision to terminate her life, her husband concluded, "It's not a matter of how long you live, but the quality of life you live, and it was her life and her decision and she chose. She made that decision based upon the fact that the things she loved most --- reading, literature, music and all that --- she couldn't do any more."

Nor is this the only such case that has arisen where the decision has been made that life is not worth living.

In Las Vegas, a 30 year old man, paralyzed from the neck down since age 10 from a swimming accident, went to court seeking the right to end his life because he feared he would outlive his terminally ill father. His mother had died of lung cancer a decade earlier. Before the court could act on his request, his father admitted giving the son Seconal and Valium, after which the father detached the respirator from his son's trachea. The father admitted he didn't want his son to die but understood his son's reasons for wanting to end his life. He concluded, "Let's face it. He's been in jail for 21 years, and I've been his keeper."

Dr. Joseph Fletcher, an Episcopal clergyman and professor emeritus of medical ethics at the University of Virginia, says it isn't clear to him that such actions violate the Hippocratic Oath, where the classic medical vow "asks the physician to promise to protect and ease the patient's suffering and also to protect the patient's life. What we're dealing with is those situations in which those two versions come into conflict." He further predicts, "One of these days, we're going to get legislation passed to allow physician-assisted suicide in cases of useless further treatment." Perhaps we will in time.

Meanwhile, what do you think? Where does the right to end life stop? In opening the proverbial "Pandora's box" by allowing individuals to assist one-another in ending their lives, as miserable as such lives may be, what limits should be established?

Exercise

1. When does a person have the right to take his/her life?

2. Under what circumstances do you feel it would be proper for someone to assist another in terminating life?

3. What restrictions, if any, would you favor applying to the use of any future invented or devised "suicide machine"?

4. Thomas Jefferson wrote, "My greatest fear is that I may live too long." What constitutes living too long for you?

5.   How would you change your response to the above question if the life at issue were not yours but the person you love most?

6.   Could you assist that family member to whom you are closest in taking his or her own life under certain conditions?   If "Yes," what are those conditions?

7.   What problems do you foresee in passing legislation permitting physicians to assist patients in their quest to end life when further treatment seems useless?

CHAPTER FIFTEEN

"Who Is Invited into Your Living Room?"

You would not think of opening the door to your home and admitting into your living room a thief, murderer, rapist, or sex offender. Indeed, we would abhor the idea of such individuals coming near us or touching in any manner the lives of those we love.

Yet, via satellite and the picture tube, nightly television fare in many homes grants such characters access to our lives, influencing our attitudes of mind and thought processes just as surely as if such persons were actually present.

"Oh, but that's just acting," we say and even when based on true stories, we conclude, "well, that's television, what else do you expect?" But shouldn't we take pains to avoid contaminating our presence or our thoughts with such negativity? And doesn't this begin by inquiring, "Just who do I invite into my living room?"

Sexual assaults have become a staple of television programs and movies. According to the

National Coalition on Television Violence based in Champaign, Illinois, one out of eight films depicts rape. Surveying preteens, the research director, Thomas Radecki, found that more adolescents could identify Jason and Freddy --- the sexually sadistic monsters appearing respectively in "Friday the I3th" and "Nightmare on Elm Street" --- than George Washington, Abraham Lincoln or Martin Luther King, Jr.!

Is it any wonder that society is experiencing such troublesome incidents involving teens and young adults when the absurd and ludicrous is offered up as normative behavior on the screens in our very own living rooms?

Emerson's warning, "We tend to become what we think about, all day long," comes to mind. We are each a product of our experiences, of all that is fed into our conscious streams of thought. And what better proof than an experiment at the University of Wisconsin? There, men who watched R-rated films were found less likely during a re-enactment of a rape to think the woman was suffering from brutalization than male subjects who hadn't seen the movies.

"It desensitizes them to the harm they're doing," says Dr. Pauline Bart, a sociologist at the University of Illinois at Chicago, a noted rape expert. Even criminal defenses have been built around the argument that the accused should not be held accountable due to too much exposure to television violence beamed into the home on a regular basis.

Studies abound suggesting that by the time children graduate from high school, many have spent more hours in front of the television set than in the classroom.   Indiscriminate TV viewing is detrimental to the health of both adults and children, given the screen's propensity to extol violence and mayhem as regular fare.

If there are young children in your home, consider the affect the programming they have seen on television today may have on their lives. Will such fare make them more secure, contribute to sound mental health, encourage them to think better of others, or to value more highly other humans and life in general?

What and who we invite into our living rooms has an on-going affect, not only on our children but on ourselves, as well. Is it for better or for worse?

Only you can decide but decide you must if you are to be a positive force for good in the lives of those you love most. Be vigilant in standing sentinel at the gateway leading to those thoughts you can influence entering their minds and cherished in their hearts. What better place to begin than with what is allowed --- nay, what is invited -- into your home via the television screen?

Exercise

1. Admitting it is more difficult today to control exposure of loved ones to harmful television fare, list several healthy means a home should consider in addressing this issue.

2. List those television programs watched in your home on a regular basis. Check with family members for any additions to the list. Using a 1 (Degrading) through 10 (Uplifting) scale, rate each of these programs.

3. If dissatisfied with the ratings assigned above, what do you plan to do about it?

4.   What are some steps you can take to assure teenage family members (or adolescents in general) are better acquainted with positive figures who influence society than with negative role models so often depicted on the screen?

5.   When it comes to feeding your mind as well as your body, do you consider one (a) as important, (b) less important, or (c) more important than the other? How do you justify your reasoning?

6.   Can a case be made showing indiscriminate television viewing as beneficial for <u>any</u> age group? Support your position.

CHAPTER SIXTEEN

"Protecting Whose Health?"

     An individual verging on death is admitted to the hospital. The attending physician makes an instant decision, necessary to address the patient's rapidly deteriorating condition, ordering an overdose of medication which when administered causes the patient to expire. Family members gather to hear the physician describe the cause of death, seeking reassurance that everything possible was done and that their loved one suffered no more than necessary. They need help in absorbing and adjusting to their initial shock of bereavement.

     If you were the physician in this instance, what would you tell family members? That there was nothing else that could be done? That the patient was so ill there was little that could have made a substantial contribution to prolonging life? Would you conclude by explaining that in light of the severity of his illness the patient had died despite your "best efforts"? Or would you admit that through an error in judgment you had contributed to his death?

     For narrowly interpreted this is true: the

physician acted within the parameters of the "best efforts" he could muster at the moment. Indeed, though obviously in error, these actions represented the finest attempt by the physician, given what was known at the time.

This hypothetical case was one of four posed ethical problems submitted to physicians by a medical panel headed by Dr. Dennis Novack, a physician at Brown University. The study's purpose was to test a doctor's responses to four ethical problems that could potentially be resolved via deception.

In the first case, 75% of responding physicians agreed that when communicating with insurance companies about patients' health coverage, they would describe a mammogram as a "diagnostic test", implying a check for at least a hint of cancer even though the test were part of a routine physical if such labeling meant the patient would receive reimbursement from the insurance carrier. Some doctors replied that a mammogram is nearly <u>always</u> appropriate, given the high incident of breast cancer, e.g., a recent study suggesting that 1 of 9 American women is expected to experience breast cancer.

Using somewhat different reasoning in the second case, nearly as high a percentage of physicians agreed that they would be party to deceiving the wife of a patient with gonorrhea if such collusion were believed necessary to keep the marriage intact. However, most would have the wife come in for treatment of "an unspecified urethritis" or infection in order to be treated for gonorrhea prevention.

In Case #3, more than half of the study's respondents, as reported in the <u>Journal of the American Medical Association</u>, said they would inform the mother of a 15-year-old that her daughter was pregnant, though the minor had explicitly asked that her parents not be informed. Interestingly though, when it came to abortion, 63% of all responding obstetricians agreed they would honor the patient's confidence.

In Case #4, to return to the overdose that resulted in the death of the patient, some physicians deciding not to admit their mistake argued that another explanation was "best for the family," as they had already suffered enough anguish. Evidently some doctors assign a higher value to their own comfort or desire to avoid a malpractice suit than to telling the surviving relatives the truth.

All of which raises the question posed at the outset: whose health is primarily being protected?

Listen to ethicist Dr. Daniel Callahan, director of the Hastings Institute for biomedical ethics. "Medicine is fallible, so doctors make errors," he said. "If there is no deliberate attempt to mislead, if no one asks, 'Did you make a mistake, doctor?' the physician does not have an obligation to hold up his hand and say, 'I made a mistake.'"

Though there is no unanimity among

physicians as to if or when doctors should lie, one underlying concern remains paramount: in cases of medical deception, is it the patient, the patient's family, or the practitioner who is being spared?

Exercise

1. How many different options confront a physician when queried by loved ones of the deceased, "What happened?" Which option do you consider preferable?

2. Were you a physician, could you imagine ever telling family members following the demise of a relative, "The mistake was mine. It was inexcusable?"

3. As a surviving family member given such explanation, how would you respond? Is there a difference in how you like to <u>think</u> you would respond?

4. When it comes to the plethora of tests available to working up a medical diagnosis, how much importance should a physician assign insurance coverage?

5. In their responsibility for providing medical care, how far do you think it proper for a physician to go in withholding information from a spouse when such knowledge could jeopardize the couple's marriage?

6. List all options available to a physician whose pregnant minor patient wants to resolve the matter herself without telling her parents. Which option do you think is preferable?

CHAPTER SEVENTEEN

"Legally Right and then Some"

Parents in our society almost universally recognize their legal obligations to their young. What they don't always so readily identify are their moral and ethical responsibilities as well, with implications extending far from the home into all aspects of life.

Whenever former Interior Secretary Donald Hodel discusses family tragedy, he speaks as a parent with first hand experience, for it was on August 7, 1974, when the Hodel's son, Philip, failed to return home for a planned birthday party.

"We had really been afraid all that summer there was going to be a knock on the door," said Barbara Hodel, struggling to hold back tears, "so the knock on the door came that night. There were two policemen on the porch and they asked us to sit down. And it wasn't of course that he had crashed the car, but that he had been found hanging from a tree." Attempting to reassure the parents, the officers told the Hodels that Philip had not been sending a plea for help but rather had intended to kill himself.

Only those families that have experienced

similar tragedies can identify with the extent of the Hodels' grief. The pained heartache, sleepless nights, cries rising from deep within themselves in the dark solitude of their bedrooms before dawn as they wonder, "What could I have done to prevent this?", have all been experienced by other parents who have confronted comparable losses.

Under such circumstances some families become bitter. Others resign themselves fatalistically falling back on the outlook, "What will be, will be." The Hodels did neither. Instead, they coped with their grief by recommitting themselves to their religious beliefs.

"We became active in the church we had fallen away from for quite some time," Donald Hodel said. "I believe," he continued, "that there would have been a much greater chance that our son could have avoided drugs if we as his parents from the early stages had understood the significance of a moral and ethical system --- in this case, of religious values --- and been diligent in training him."

How many parents harbor the same lament, even though they have not faced tragedy of a similar nature? One can only wonder when considering the unwillingness of so many mothers and fathers to confront moral and ethical responsibilities as diligently as they do the legal ones affecting their children.

Obviously moral and ethical responsibilities apply to the individual as well as to the family. They are also found in the corporate world.

However, former Chamber of Commerce Chairman William S. Kanaga notes, "Mere obedience to rules and laws is not enough. Legality must be a floor, not a ceiling. If management conveys a sense of corner-cutting or minimal conformity, the employees will embrace that standard across the board."

Nepotism, the hiring of relatives, is generally regarded a gray area where there is no specific company prohibition against the practice. Legally speaking, nepotism may not present a problem, but what about ethically?

Luther Hodges, former Secretary of Commerce and previously governor of North Carolina, described his approach to going beyond what was legally required when he served as a general manager with Marshall Field's, where 4,000 employees reported to him. In his geographical area lived seven of Hodges' eight brothers and sisters with their families. There was little opportunity for work other than in the mills. Yet, Hodges writes that he made a point of never bringing a single member of his family into his office to discuss a job and never interceded for any of them. Not one was ever placed on the payroll by him nor as a result of his influence. Nor did he ever interfere when one was hired, fired, transferred or refused employment by the personnel office.

Many times he may have acted legally had he taken an active role regarding the disposition of a matter involving a relative. Yet, Hodges felt that morally he had an obligation that went <u>beyond</u> what would have been considered legal.

In choosing to do what is right in interacting with another, wouldn't we be better off were we to consider what is legally right as the floor, i.e., the starting point of acceptable behavior? For then we would be positioned to shift to ethical excellence, moving beyond what is legally right to consider instead what is <u>morally right</u>.

Exercise

1. What is it about society that makes us more aware of the legal than of the ethical implications of our behavior?

2. How can we increase parental awareness regarding the importance of what they teach their children ethically?

3. What role does religious activity play in underscoring the importance of making ethical choices (a) at home, and (b) in the business world?

5.   A radio commentator recently stated, "I'd lie, cheat and steal for my young and I hope they'd do the same for me." How far would you go to bend rules to benefit a family member?

6.   Can a case ever be made that nepotism falls outside the realm of ethical behavior?

7.   What examples come to mind that are legally right though morally wrong?

CHAPTER EIGHTEEN

"Learning to Discern a Benefit for All"

Themes of drug abuse, violence, sexual immorality, suicide and the occult often appear not only in the movies adolescents rent, but also in the musical lyrics of the tapes they purchase. The concern, says former disc jockey, Bob DeMoss, "[is when] children are blitzed with these messages, how can they learn to discern proper behavior? Too often, kids become desensitized..."

One example are the lyrics in "As Nasty As They Wanna Be" by 2 Live Crew, where more than 100 references are made to male and female genitalia, including more than a dozen illustrations of violent sexual abuse of the female. How do younger family members learn to discern between good and bad, desirable and undesirable when exposed to such fare?

Or note the album, "Niggaz4life," by the rap group N.W.A. Shortly after its debut the album rose to No. 1 on Billboard magazine pop charts, though the violence chronicled goes far beyond that of 2 Live Crew. Topical reference is made to killing, mutilating, raping and making women do sex acts against their will. The album's message is one of wanton meanness and is dehumanizing. Yet, it seems safe to assume that at least some parents are aware of what their children are buying and what they are listening to, even outside the home.

In other instances what goes on in the home makes it difficult for family members to distinguish between preferable and non-preferable behavior.

Take the case of Coupon Connie, who was known to bring home $300 worth of groceries for little more than $8 plus wads of cents-off coupons. Trading coupons with others pursuing similar ends, eventually she was charged with scheming to buy and sell thousands of counterfeit rebate coupons.

Of course another angle is that worked by unscrupulous merchants who send in coupons for reimbursement without ever making the sale, profiting from "cents off" of a product that has never left the shelf. But back to coupon collectors and manufacturers.

Says attorney Len Perkins, "Some offers require receipts, and some people go so far as to have their own cash registers to print them up." When rebates are limited to one per customer, often people try and get around this stipulation by using multiple post office boxes.

Others jumble their names into anagrams and fudge the digits in their addresses, hoping to circumvent company limits on the number of coupons allotted each household. Says Judith Farrell, a coupon expert with the A. C. Nielsen Clearing House, "You'd be surprised at the variations you can create out of a single name and address. It sounds like a lot of trouble for a few bucks, but it adds up fast."

Now back to Coupon Connie. Eventually she began buying coupons from a man in Texas, who was offering some that could be exchanged for free food. You could take your pick: any 10 items for $7.50. After buying coupons for sometime, Connie began to deal by buying the coupons for 25 cents, then reselling them for twice that.

When postal inspectors investigated the coupon scheme, they wondered if it were normal for a housewife to buy 5,000 to 10,000 coupons for $200 or $300, when they were actually worth $2,000 to $3,000. Said one, "Wouldn't she obviously know something was wrong?"

In the midst of all this was the trader's young daughter, who had to question what was going on. Truly it is difficult to argue that her Mother's role-play has done much to help the daughter make positive choices when it comes to making ethical decisions affecting her life.

Exercise

1. Can children or youth learn to discern between the desirable and undesirable in homes that pander to lust and violence in film and lyrics? Explain.

2. Thinking back over the past few years, in what areas have you become desensitized due to a blitzing or overexposure affecting your senses?

3. What examples in the home come to mind that <u>help</u> young people discern good from bad?

4.   At what point do you think most people would recognize the foodstuffs coupon scheme as obviously illegal?

5.   What rationalizing would buyers draw on to justify using their own cash registers to match receipts with coupons?

6.   Who was the role-model who helped you most in learning to discern between right and wrong in your own decision making?

7.   In what ways do you strive to emulate this role-model, recognizing that you also serve as a role model --- directly or indirectly --- for others?

CHAPTER NINETEEN

"Can Safe Sex be Assured?"

A recent survey of 422 sexually active University of Southern California college students reveals that asking one's partner about his or her sex history is no guarantee of safe sex. One third of the men and 10 percent of the women admitted they had lied to a partner in order to have sex.

So much for one's word improving the likelihood of safe sex. Yet, in and out of marriage, individuals often rely on one another's truthfulness as to the likelihood of the partner being a carrier of an infectious disease. Verbal assurance is, of course, frequently unreliable, as many can attest.

A couple with three children had been married for 12 years. In the last two years she had experienced occasional facial lesions but thought little of them at the time. After a particularly troublesome vaginal infection she was informed by her gynecologist that she tested positive for HIV-1, the HIV-virus that causes AIDS.

Her doctor tactfully inquired of her sexual partners. "This can't be," she exclaimed, "I have been absolutely monogamous --- without question," she added for emphasis, "<u>throughout our marriage</u>."

Then like a bolt from the blue she thought of her husband. "It <u>has</u> to be him," she reasoned. At first he denied any extramarital sexual involvement. Desperate to believe him, she clung to his assurance emotionally, though intellectually she knew better.

Two weeks later he confessed that, yes, he had been seeing a woman from work for nearly three years. However, he didn't think the woman had been unfaithful to him during this time! Yet, the sexual histories of <u>any</u> of the three had a direct bearing on the possibility <u>and</u> probability of each contracting an infectious sexual disease.

When consenting to sexual activity an individual is essentially going to bed not only with a specific partner, but with everyone with whom the partner has ever slept. The mathematical possibilities of exposure grow exponentially and are virtually unlimited when one considers multiple partners, each of whom has had multiple partners.

So how can you assure safe sex? There is simply no substitute for insisting on latex condom usage during coitus (and even then use of condoms is no guarantee of safe sex). However, short of abstinence, this is the <u>best</u> available means of assuring safe sex.

To depend on the truthfulness of a potential sex partner's verbal assurances is risky, as psychologists Dr. Susan D. Cochran and Dr. Vickie M. Mays, who conducted the USC study, found when they queried Southern California college students, getting them to answer anonymous questionnaires on lying and sex. In addition to 4 percent of the women stating they would lie about positive results on a blood test for the AIDS virus, an alarming 20 percent of the men professed no qualms in this regard. In the same study, 47 percent of the men and 42 percent of the women said they would understate the number of their sexual partners.

Other sexual differences were also discovered. For instance, men were less likely than women to confess to infidelity or to inform a partner that they were also seeing someone else. When quizzed specifically, 65 percent of the men and 61 percent of the women reported they would tell a partner about another relationship only "when [it seemed] safe to do so" or "if asked."

If any conclusion can be extrapolated from such a study, it would seem prudent to insist on something more than another's verbal assurance in pursuing safe sex.

Exercise

1. Under what conditions would you be willing to accept another's word in the pursuit of "safe sex"?

2. How do you account for the marked discrepancy (20 percent male, 4 percent female) who would lie that they had tested positive for the HIV-1, the HIV-virus that causes AIDS?

3. Why aren't more people hesitant to accept another's word regarding sexual practices, past or current?

4. What is the justification for concluding that someone who is being unfaithful to another will not in turn be unfaithful to you?

5. Draw a diagram showing how many people's sexual histories are intertwined where each of three individuals involved sexually have been involved with three other persons who have been sexually engaged with three additional people.

6. Using the above diagram, illustrate how in only seven "sexual generations" 2,187 sexual histories are involved.

7.   Why do you suppose men seem far more likely than women to lie about their results on blood tests for the AIDS producing virus?

CHAPTER TWENTY

"Whom Can You Trust?"

Homewreckers are forever the bane of troubled marital relationships. The other woman, the other man, those who seemingly lie in wait to prey on dissatisfied spouses, have been described in literature throughout recorded history. So what else is new?

The difference is that today many marriages require two incomes, necessitating that both partners find employment in the work place outside the home. Obviously greater opportunities abound for sexual indiscretions when both husband and wife are exposed on a daily basis to many people in their jobs.

But even more threatening is the amoral or immoral professional sought out by a troubled spouse during a crisis. Such abuse is not unknown, whether the specialist has been trained in the field of medicine, psychology, theology, or law.

One couple's marriage had not gone well for months. Finally they decided to seek professional help. She called, making an appointment with a marriage counselor. Both spouses showed up for the first session.

After several sessions of therapy the

husband felt the emotional distance between the couple was even greater than before. Soon he discovered his wife was seeing the therapist outside of their sessions. When confronted, she admitted she had been having an affair with their counselor for two months.

Devastated emotionally, the husband sued the psychotherapist, charging malpractice and intentional infliction of emotional distress based on the therapist having advised the husband to stay away from his wife. Eventually the therapist married this former client, but the suit continues, with the state high court having ruled there is sufficient cause to proceed in that the therapist "...was not the milkman, the mailman or the guy next door." Indeed, he was a trusted professional, whom the husband contends misplaced the trust the couple had initially deposited in him.

A New York lawyer, charged with having an affair with a client who had come to him to file divorce proceedings is appealing a $10,000 fine a judge levied against him for his misconduct and for not removing himself from the case because of a sexual liaison with his client. Surprisingly, unlike psychiatrists and psychologists, whose professional associations ethically proscribe them from sleeping with patients, lawyers have generally been left on their own to interpret their professional deportment in regard to their clients.

The problem, of course, is that clients in

the throes of emotional upheaval are vulnerable and easily manipulated by professionals to whom they have turned as sources of help precisely for their professionalism and objective input.

Nor are parishioners necessarily safe when it comes to sexual exploitation. Certain church members are most susceptible to cleric Lotharios, whom psychiatrist Dr. Glenn Gabbard, director of the Menninger Hospital in Topeka, Kansas, describes as "longing to be loved, to be idealized, to be godlike."

Where a woman consults a clergyman who is burned out and troubled by his own low self-image and frailties, choosing to deposit her total trust and acceptance in him, the minister's "original wish to be loved like God is", according to Gabbard, causes him to be vulnerable to a sexual liaison. "In these situations," he continues, "women may well imagine that a sexual union with [such a lofty figure] is going to have a tremendous benefit." Of course it doesn't.

Betrayal of persons' confidences by taking advantage of them when they are most vulnerable emotionally is often referred to as "authority rape". When a sacred trust is violated victims look for someone or something to blame. Some turn on themselves, some on the professional calling of the offender, while others, particularly in clergy-parishioner situations, blame God.

Determining whom you can trust is difficult, especially when in a moment of crisis and trauma you may be most vulnerable to being used and abused. Avoiding being preyed upon at such a time may require seeking another opinion or input from a different professional at the first <u>hint</u> of even a scintilla of suggestion that your trust may be about to be violated.

Exercise

1. What criteria would an individual confronting a life crisis best be advised to follow in seeking professional consultation?

2. Why do you think patients or clients stick with professionals they feel may be abusing them while purportedly seeking to help them?

3. What case can be made for a professional beginning a relationship outside treatment or consultations with a client/patient/parishioner?

4. Would the public's best interest be served if the American Bar Association specifically <u>proscribed</u> sexual relations between clients and attorneys? Explain.

5. What steps should religious denominations take to eliminate so far as possible the potential for sexual abuse in pastor/parishioner relationships?

6. Why are some persons seemingly more vulnerable than others to "authority rape", where the perpetrator is assigned a lofty image by the victim?

PART III.

Applying Ethics in

BUSINESS

PART III.

"Applying Ethics in BUSINESS"

Does good ethics = good business? Obviously some corporations think so.

For the last eight years General Motors has spent an estimated $3.5 billion developing a new, sporty Saturn sedan to compete primarily with quality foreign cars which have attracted larger numbers of American buyers each year. Imagine the concern of GM executives when dealers around the country began reporting leaks and corrosion in the cooling systems of cars produced between March 25 and April 4, 1991, at the company's lone Spring Hill, Tennessee plant.

An investigation uncovered 54 barrels of premixed coolant provided Saturn by a major oil company. The mixture contained improperly high levels of caustic agents, with the antifreeze eating through component parts of the cooling system. Reportedly, 1,836 cars with faulty coolant mixtures had been shipped, of which dealers had sold 1,100 when the mistake was discovered.

Rather than recalling the cars solely for repair of the coolant systems, General Motors announced it would replace all faulty Saturns sold, as well as those on dealer lots. This went far beyond the usual practice in the auto industry of recalling cars and offering to repair only the damaged systems free of charge. Describing its decision to replace rather than to recall these cars, company officials termed the action a "customer satisfaction campaign."

Good ethics? But of course. Good business? What else? The rewards will be real for GM, as its decision represents ethics in action at its best. Simply put, many would agree it's <u>The Right Thing</u>.

Yet in all too many instances personal ethical teachings seem to be set aside when an opportunity to apply these same standards arises in business. No institution nor business area in corporate America seems immune from such practices of ethics inaction.

Education practices come under continual attack, either for promoting and graduating students ill-equipped to participate in the work world or for protecting incompetent professionals from being replaced. And can the role of athletics in these instances of ethical lapses be over-emphasized?

For instance, booster clubs exist in some large urban high schools. When the NCAA turned its attention to Atlanta's Southside Comprehensive High School, it discovered a student who graduated and enrolled at Clemson University but who hadn't met certain high school academic requirements. The matter has triggered separate investigations into possible recruitment violations, altered transcripts and misuse of booster club funds at the high school.

In this particular case, the student left a small school system in Tennessee after finishing the 10th grade, moving in and living in the home of an assistant basketball coach at Atlanta's Southside. An outstanding athlete, evidently the student took special-education classes and not enough standard curriculum courses to meet NCAA eligibility requirements.

An on-going investigation reports evidence that some Southside athletes received credit for courses not taken. Others had their grades and transcripts altered. Some are even suspected of having been "brokered" to specific colleges for unspecified compensation.

We've long heard of such problems at the college level. But in high schools?

Though the NCAA serves as a policing agent for colleges and universities, high schools are left virtually on their own to run their sports programs. Is it possible that problems are greater than perceived, even by those knowledgeable of existing situations at secondary school levels around the country?

Nor are academic communities, per se, immune when applying ethics corporately. Higher educational institutions have been rocked by allegations of multimillion-dollar "gamesmanship" pitting universities against the government which underwrites the bulk of research grants. Rather than athletics as an issue, it is the more lofty sector --- research --- often considered immune from such ethical lapses, that has found itself at the eye of the storm.

When federal officials audited various research programs they discovered that a dozen higher education institutions had improperly written off more than $14 million as expenses relating to federal research. Claims submitted listed these expenses as eligible for government reimbursement.

Said Richard Kusserow, inspector general of the Health and Human Services Department, "The purpose of this money [research grants]...is to advance science. We should not be subsidizing the university for its normal operations."

A House subcommittee has been informed that irregularities were discovered at twelve schools, where entertainment expenses, funds for catered affairs and personal housing, among other things, had been included as overhead costs directly related to funded research.

Bills submitted relating to research that have since been denied government reimbursement include air fare to Grand Cayman Island for a university president's wife; engraved crystal decanters from upscale Neiman Marcus; a sculpture, already paid for by a university donor, and in one instance a 72-foot yacht!

Nor are the schools involved small or unknown academic institutions. Rather, many are among the nation's most elite. In some instances top administrators have resigned.

Other institutions forced to make ethical decisions unique to these economic times include public libraries, where many homeless congregate, especially on cold days. What rights exist for use of these facilities by those whose body odors and general health offend others?

When the Joint Free Public Library of Morristown and Morris Township in New Jersey challenged the presence of such patrons, they, in turn, were challenged by the ACLU, which argued in court that such a ban violates First Amendment protections and other rights.

Though attorneys for the library argue that these institutions are not equipped to handle the homeless and are ill-equipped to serve as "adult babysitters", what inherent ethical implications are presented for tax supported institutions, to say nothing of tax-payers?

Or what are the ethical ramifications for

hospitals and medical centers, where funds are not available for every need. Where can the line be drawn? Where should it be drawn?

Hennepin County Medical Center in Minneapolis is a high-tech facility, where a patient, Helga Wanglie, age 87, was kept alive in its intensive care unit solely by a feeding tube and a ventilator. Claiming the treatment administered for more than a year was futile, the hospital sought permission to take the patient off these life supports.

The patient suffered from extensive brain damage following cardiac arrest in a nursing home. Her husband, Oliver, 87, refused to authorize the removal of the life support systems. The hospital asked a judge to appoint a guardian who could authorize removal of the ventilator.

Though this may be the first case where a hospital went to court seeking permission to terminate patient care against family wishes, it will hardly be the last. Before the patient expired, medical expenses came close to $1 million dollars. Monies simply aren't available to provide all the assistance family members might desire. Again, where is the line to be drawn?

Here, we have the specific issue of how far an institution should go in providing care demanded by a patient's family when medical authorities do not feel such care will be beneficial. These problems can be expected to mushroom as the 70 percent of Medicaid costs that already go to care for elderly nursing home patients is substantially increased.

How much is too much health care provided geriatric patients in their declining years? What are the implications for other sectors of society, where funds are desperately needed, i.e., crack babies, pregnant women who receive inadequate care, psychological, psychiatric, and social services for emotionally disturbed persons roaming streets in our major cities? These are but a few of such issues we must face collectively.

In the corporate world it is also easy to go astray ethically in the quest to be competitive. For instance, cholesterol is presently a major issue in marketing all types of food products. The Food and Drug Administration has warned several companies about labels it feels mislead consumers.

In cases involving Procter & Gamble's Crisco vegetable oil claim of "No Cholesterol", as well as that of Mazola corn oil and Heartbeat canola oil, the agency argued that it is misleading for companies to claim these products contain no cholesterol when cholesterol is a substance found only in animal products, **not** in vegetable oils.

Going a step further, rather than being heart healthy, these oils contain entirely too much fat. Labels and product claims tell only part of the story when we realize that saturated fats in many oils, including corn oil and canola oil, have been implicated in heart disease and cancer.

Though the claim "No Cholesterol" to describe vegetable oils is not false, is it ethical to mislead or to attempt to redirect public attention away from other properties in a product that could be as hazardous to consumers' health?

And are these cited industries largely recognized as among those most likely to pursue ethics inaction? Of course not. Their ethical lapses are just that: lapses --- <u>temporary lapses</u> --- which afflict individuals and corporations at every turn. What is needed is constant vigilance to assure not that the lower but rather that the higher ethical road is sought and taken at every turn.

Corporate ethics in action are easily discernible in financial fields, where facts tend to be more objective, though some rightfully argue this isn't <u>always</u> so. In recent months the far-flung Bank of Credit and Commerce International (BCCI) has come under investigation in nearly every country where it does business. Concerns focus on drug cartel financial dealings, as well as handling other tainted money transactions.

Interest in the nation's capital has focused on BCCI having obtained secret ownership in a holding company that owned a major Washington bank, First American Bank, though assurance was given repeatedly by some of the more venerable business personalities in the city that there was absolutely no BCCI involvement in this institution. Congressional hearings will examine what involvement existed and any subsequent ramifications of an internationally scandalized corporation secretly buying major financial institutions in this country.

Meanwhile, sterling reputations of men who have left their mark serving in high posts in administrations and involved in all manner of good works in Washington are on the line. How do business leaders and the companies they head stray from a course of ethics in action to the less desirable one of ethics inaction?

Famed Salomon Brothers, Inc., one of Wall Street's oldest and most prominent investment firms, has been rocked by scandal, causing the resignations of leaders in the firm. Acknowledged violations in trading in U. S. government bond auctions by attempting to monopolize the market and then to resell these securities at a premium surfaced after the May, 1991 auction was held, where $12.25 billion dollars of two-year notes were sold. By allegedly trading in its own account and in filling orders for firms without the latters' knowledge, Salomon apparently cornered more goverment securities than is legally permissible.

Aside from jeopardizing local trust in the United States government's ability to conduct honest financial auctions, concern is heightened regarding international faith in this country's ability to continue operating in a straight-forward manner that will guarantee multiple bidders coming forward, keeping the borrowing rate of the federal government and, yes, of each and every one of us, as low as possible. All of which stems from the problem of a major financial firm going astray and in a moment of ethics inaction destroying a reputation built over the years of being one of the nation's stalwart institutions where ethics in action was considered normative.

These examples underscore the problem recent polls have highlighted, e.g., when reporting that nationwide in the past decade the Savings and Loans industry and banking institutions in general have suffered a marked loss of respect. Within the United States, literally billions have been added to the national debt by individuals and financial institutions violating laws and dealing unethically with their stockholders and the general public.

Falsifying financial documents and exceeding limits on loans to directors are just two practices costing the Federal Deposit Insurance Corporation $160 million, a figure many knowledgeable sources claim will prove conservative. In some instances, failed institutions had ties to officials in the Office of the Comptroller of the Currency (OCC). One investigation by a congressional committee found that a top official of a failed institution admitted making calls to his connections within OCC, though he denied having ever spoken with his wife --- a senior OCC administrator --- about the problem.

Many of these financial problems stem from real estate investments that have gone sour, a chief cause of much of the monetary morass experienced by lending institutions at the start of this, the final decade of the 20th century. As loan security, land assessed at far more than it was worth was often put up as collateral for increased leverage. When the market for unimproved land evaporated, institutions were deluged with bad debt.

Not that unethical behavior is responsible for **all** woes of financial institutions. Still, we must wonder which institutions now insolvent would be solvent today had a corporate ethic prevailed causing these institutions to choose to do what was right --- The Right Thing --- whenever tempted to act otherwise. Had such options been relentlessly pursued, would these corporations be better off? Would individuals at all levels within these companies have benefitted?

And what about the general public, which through taxation will shoulder the brunt of these losses? Would the standard of living in the United States be improved were we not saddled with such debt?

At the same time, many individuals of conscience and institutions where high ethical standards are the norm can be found throughout the corporate world. In fact, it is a safe assumption that there are far more ethical than unethical individuals and companies around. Were this not so, ethical inaction such as described above would not make news. In fact, were it commonplace, ethics inaction at the corporate level wouldn't rate so much as an inch of newsprint.

As further proof of the value of pursuing ethics in action in business, listen to Empire Southwest's CEO, Jack Whiteman, when he notes, "There is no doubt in my mind that ethical behavior pays off at the bottom line." His firm gets 60% of the projects it bids and whenever all things are equal, customers frequently give Empire Southwest benefit of any doubt, so well known is the company for its pursuit of ethics in action. Will more corporate leaders tend to do the right thing when presented with future ethical alternatives?

More and more stockholders are refusing to remain aloof from the fray of ethics inaction versus ethics in action. Whether or not you agree with their goals, social policy shareholder proposals have had a major impact on the nation's corporations, according to the Investor Responsibility Research Center of Washington. In 1991 proposals asking management to cut ties to South Africa won an average of 13 percent of the votes at the annual meetings of 81 banks and industrial companies, representing an all time high.

In addition, shareholders seeking corporate support for the MacBride Principles, which beseech companies to observe fair employment practices in strife-filled Northern Ireland, won almost 11 percent of the vote at 18 companies. And the Valdez Principles, a tough environmental code of conduct for corporations, received an average vote of 8 percent at 24 companies asked to sign the principles.

Resolutions aimed at curbing seven tobacco company advertising and marketing programs by shareholders received 4.7 percent of the vote, a better result than a year ago. And though these percentages may not seem all that impressive, they represent ripple effects that will reverberate in policy decisions of corporations directly and indirectly affected by these votes for years to come.

Corporate ethics in action: it's not a new story in American business. Some years ago Minnesota Mining and Manufacturing (3M) won plaudits for its "Pollution Prevention Pays" initiative, designed to eliminate pollutants from the manufacturing process at the outset rather than attacking these problems after the fact (and this long before environmental issues became as prominent as they are today).

In another effort to affect the environment, 3M was among the first companies to install a fleet of commuter vans, starting with but six vans in 1973. Numerous other corporations have similar programs today, all stemming from ethical decisions to affect positively the environment and the quality of life in urban areas by reducing the number of vehicles depositing daily pollutants into the atmosphere.

Cummins Engine is a firm also highly regarded for its on-going practice of ethics in action in business. Executives having made ethical decisions costly to the firm are legend, inspired in no small manner by the example set by Cummins' former CEO,

J. Irwin Miller, who has been honored numerous times by humanitarian and religious organizations for his exemplary ethical leadership. Further evidence of Cummins Engine's developed corporate conscience is observed when noting the company gives five percent of its domestic pretax profits to charity each year.

Beatrice Foods came to prominence for ethical decision making and leadership in its role of aiding food banks, helping to feed the homeless in America. Second Harvest, a hunger relief organization, has benefitted as part of an extensive network of food banks in America. Much of the funding for this and similar programs has come from Beatrice.

Clorox is yet another ethical corporation cited for its support for youth programs in economically depressed Oakland, California, home of its corporate headquarters. Its East Oakland Youth Development Center (EOYDC) job training and counseling facility has had a tremendous impact for good in a neighborhood where over 50 percent of the families lived at or below the poverty level. Clorox has invested heavily in programs operated through this center even extending its youth program, awarding grants to develop youth-oriented projects to company plants in other cities. And several years ago when many corporations were deserting cities for suburban settings, Clorox chose a counter-course, locating its new offices in downtown Oakland.

The ability of the individual of conscience to influence his/her workplace environment cannot be over-stated. Examining how the plans for Trump Tower in New York City fell into place is illustrative of this point.

After acquiring needed air rights from Bonwit and Equitable, Donald Trump needed one more: those of Tiffany. Meeting with Walter Hoving, Tiffany's owner, Trump offered to buy these air rights for $5 million dollars. Hoving agreed, but was going away with his wife for a month. The necessary papers would be signed upon Hoving's return.

Trump protested, afraid Hoving would change his mind, but Hoving assured him, "...perhaps you don't understand. I shook your hand. I made a deal with you. That's that."

Imagine Trump's nervousness while Hoving was gone. First, Philip Morris bought air rights over Grand Central paying far more than Trump had agreed to pay for Tiffany's Fifth Avenue air rights. Then Avon agreed to buy Tifanny's but as a condition Avon wanted Hoving to include the air-rights he had agreed to sell Trump.

Tiffany executives met with Mr. Hoving upon his return, informing him of what had transpired. They suggested Tiffany might be better served were the earlier agreement with Trump negated.

Responded Hoving, "Gentlemen...I shook hands with [Trump] over a month ago. When I make a deal, that's the deal, whether it's a good one or a bad one. And I trust I won't have to explain myself again." Supposedly he didn't.

Here was a business dealing that could have gone awry at several points due to better opportunities for the seller. That it didn't was solely due to the impeccable integrity of Walter Hoving.

Good neighbors --- good citizens --- good employers, all are adjectives descriptive of corporate America at its best.

Case studies in the following section explore ways The Right Thing will be chosen even more often as individuals who have personally and interpersonally applied high ethical standards increasingly influence and help direct corporate America to take stands favoring the harder right over the easier wrong.

CHAPTER TWENTY-ONE

"More Honorable Choices In Business"

Vendor bids are important in any construction firm's project proposal. Since the goal is to submit a profitable bid, the task is to keep the contracted price attractive and competitive enough to cause the firm to be awarded the contract. Good business? Of course. It is also good stewardship.

For instance: should the lowest vendor bid <u>always</u> be accepted? What is the responsibility of the primary bidder when a vendor's bid comes in so much lower than others that it is apparent the vendor will lose money, possibly going under financially?

Such an ethical dilemma was encountered by Robert George, CEO of Medallion Construction Company in Merrimack, New Hampshire. As the prime contractor bidding on a 2.5 million dollar public housing project, Medallion received a bid submitted by a local electrical subcontractor that appeared to George to be 20 percent too low when compared with quotes from four other subcontractors.

Rather than immediately accepting the

bid containing the subcontractor's obvious error, George pondered his choices. Was it ethical to use figures he knew would result in serious cost overruns for the sub? What was Medallion's responsibility to the subcontractor? Should George just keep quiet? Such was Medallion's ethical dilemma.

Phoning the low bidder, George said, "Look I'm not going to tell you what your competitors bid, but your number is very low --- in my opinion, too low." The subcontractor withdrew his bid. Even so, Medallion was awarded the large contract.

A year later this same subcontractor bid on another of Medallion's projects. "He was offering me a two percent discount off the street price," said George, "because he said he remembered how I had treated him a year earlier. . . .It showed me that when you do something positive it comes back to you in a positive way."

Valuing long-term over short-term gain obviously paid off for George. Foregoing an immediate ill-gained (due to his recognition of the ridiculously low bid submitted earlier by the vendor) smaller profit, ultimate payoff benefitted all three parties. This can be examined as a "Triple Win" situation.

First, Robert George, the CEO, had to feel good about himself. He had made an ethical decision, one that he knew was right. The old axiom, "A sleeping pill is a poor substitute for a guilty conscience," was not one to concern George. He could rest easy. Thereafter he could look at himself in the mirror each morning as he shaved, unencumbered by anxiety over having mistreated another. By taking such ethical action, he had freed himself henceforth to tackle constructively the tasks of the day.

Next, the Medallion Construction Company was rewarded financially when the vendor expressed his gratitude for George's consideration by deliberately underbidding his subcontracting services on this second project. The vendor's largess obviously had a positive affect on Medallion's bottom line profit. Further, the company's reputation for corporate integrity was enhanced, undoubtedly leading other subcontractors and major firms to conclude that Medallion is a good corporation with which to do business, especially as the vendor spread the story of how a business Goliath had looked out for a David.

Finally, the vendor was saved from disaster because someone cared. A more honorable choice had been made, one with far reaching ramifications which the vendor in his undying gratitude would --- nay, could --- never forget. To all who would forever listen, the vendor had a message: "There's profit in virtue, especially in applying high ethical standards to business practices." Robert George of Medallion Construction was, of course, a prime example.

Coming full-cycle, for George's company, Medallion, as the popular song refrain proclaims --- "Who could ask for anything more?"

Though we may not be corporate executives confronting similar ethical dilemmas to those George faced, each of us is challenged to <u>make more honorable choices</u> daily. Determining what these are and how we will respond to them involves far reaching implications affecting both the present and the future.

Exercise

1. Is "good business" always "good stewardship"?
    What examples come to mind?

2. What ethical case can be made for <u>not</u> going with
    the lowest bid?

3. List several options from which a contractor must
    choose when a vendor's sub-contract appears too
    low.

4. Which of these options is preferable? Why?

5. When George phoned the subcontractor informing him his bid was too low, he was treating the vendor ethically. What case can be made for George's ethical treatment of his own company --- Medallion?

6. Doing something positive doesn't <u>always</u> pay off, as we all know. Still, list positive things you have done that have paid off.

7. Cite every example you can recall that in business, "Ethics pays."

CHAPTER TWENTY-TWO

"When Integrity is the Missing Link"

But an occasional glance at the sports page suggests that all is not right in collegiate athletics. Regularly some new infraction of National Collegiate Athletic Association (NCAA) rules surfaces, involving some of the better known college and university programs.

When a press conference was held to introduce the University of Oklahoma coach --- whose primary mission presumably was to restore the Sooners pride, newly installed Coach Gary Gibbs said, "All we've got to do is the right thing." No one could argue with that.

In fact, doesn't each of us feel compelled to do the right thing in most instances? If so, why is it that we so often fail to exercise ethical choices when making decisions? Why is integrity frequently the missing link, not only concerning individual, but corporate choices, as well?

Few are unaware of recent ethical difficulties involving certain Wall Street firms. The list of misdeeds is long and has been well chronicled. In one instance brokers were led from the trading center in handcuffs, leading one wag to predict that the modern childhood game of cops and robbers will henceforth take a new twist: instead of "cops and robbers" it will now be known as "cops and brokers"!

But to be fair, occasional lapses in integrity occur with some regularity in nearly all businesses, spilling over into the lives of most individuals, as well.

Sometimes a lapse of integrity involves both corporate policy as well as key individuals in their roles as company officers. Such may have been the case two decades ago with Sears, Roebuck & Co. --- though generally widely recognized for its integrity --- when it experienced at best a temporary lapse in ethical conduct concerning its relations with a Mr. Peter Roberts.

Roberts, then a clerk at a Sears outlet in Gardner, Massachusetts, had invented a quick-release wrench, a push button tool permitting removal of sockets from the device with one hand. Perhaps you have seen or used such a tool.

Since Roberts had invented this tool on his own time he was awarded a patent for it in 1965. Convinced by his employer that his invention was only of minor importance, Roberts accepted a payment of $10,000 from the corporate giant for rights to his patent.

Later while serving in the United States Air Force, Roberts noticed a big display ad for the tool in a Sears catalog. Investigating, he found that Sears had sold 19 million of these wrenches between 1965 and 1975 for a net profit of more than $44 million dollars!

Roberts sued to break the earlier agreement, as he felt he had been misled regarding the true worth of his invention. Eventually he was awarded a settlement in federal court that totaled $8.2 million dollars.

The giant merchandiser appealed, but two days into the final trial both sides settled. Presumably Roberts became much the richer at Sears expense.

Such a tale involves more than a mere David taking on a Goliath and winning. Where, you might wonder, was that ethical man or woman in the hierarchy at Sears a quarter-century ago whose voice once raised against this injustice could have prevailed, causing the giant merchandizing firm to right a wrong?

Better still, where are those voices calling out today that could make a difference in other cases as blatantly unfair? Are they sought in vain?

Most of us look outside ourselves hoping someone else will be responsible and do what is right. What we fail to see is that lapses in integrity abound, with the temptations all but overwhelming. Thus,rather than looking for someone else to take a stand, what is needed is for you and me to listen to that small voice within bridging the gap when integrity is lacking. For, all things considered, integrity is seldom a constant.

Of course some will argue integrity is but a matter of perceptions, though were it possible to reduce integrity in this manner, would there be any who would argue that perceptions are <u>unimportant</u>?

Professor John Pearce surveyed 131 college business majors. His finding? By a 2 to 1 ratio students judged the climate in American business to be essentially unethical. Further, half of these students expected that during their own business careers they would engage in behavior that is less than ethical.

Perhaps Dr. Abraham Zaleznik, a psychoanalyst affiliated with the Harvard Business School, sums it up best when he notes, "Conscience is a fragile thing. It needs support from institutions and that support is weakening." Corporations need to offer support systems buoying up the individual conscience --- and ultimately the collective conscience.

Meanwhile, as individuals, we need to apply an ethical yardstick to our actions else we run the danger of becoming ensnared in a mire of decisions arrived at when our own integrity is less than what it should be, representing a missing link in our moral codes.

For the loser in such instances is not only the individual but the corporation as well.

Exercise

1. Is it more difficult: (1) to determine or (2) to do the right thing? Cite examples supporting your position.

2. Do you feel most businesses try to do what's right? What are some factors making it difficult for companies to choose the harder right over the easier wrong?

3. Who finds ethical decisions most difficult: the individual or the corporation? Why?

4. Had Sears initially believed Roberts' invention not to be revolutionary, at what point should they have contacted him to renegotiate a contract that was generating far more money than had been anticipated?

5. What were Roberts' ethical options once he had signed the agreement accepting a $10,000 payment for his invention?

6. Do you think it likely you will be called on in the future to engage in unethical practices or conduct? If your answer is "Yes," how do you think you will respond?

CHAPTER TWENTY-THREE

"Your Conscience: Asleep or at Work?"

"Let your conscience be your guide." Good advice, right? After all, shouldn't you be able to depend on that small inner voice within when making decisions, big or small?

Sometimes upon "hearing" that inner voice warning you to stay away from some forbidding but desirable goal there is the temptation to inquire, "Who said that?" Then when the little voice says, "This is your conscience speaking," we are all too likely to respond, "Who?"

Of course your reaction will depend almost solely on your response to the question: "How well developed is your conscience?" For some the answer is, "It could be better developed." Then there are those who appear to have no consciences whatsoever. Such individuals may be young or old, though there is evidence of a growing problem of what is best defined as "limited" conscience development among younger segments of the population.

In Manteca, California, for instance, a 13-year-old boy confessed to going to a friend's house where he helped ambush the friend's father in his own home. The father was kicked, stabbed, and beaten with a fireplace poker before being choked to death with a dog chain.

Even street-hardened police were affected by such a heinous crime. One officer inquired, "Why did you pour salt in the victim's wounds?" With a shrug, one of the youngsters replied, "Oh, I don't know. I just seen it on TV."

But youth aside, adult conscience lapses are legion, too. And yes, in light of some recent events we may wonder if certain adult consciences are any more highly developed than those found among some youth.

Examples abound in the daily news, including the principal arrested for buying crack near his apartment, a teacher caught snorting cocaine in the school parking lot or administrators at a masonry institute, who promised food and job training to homeless people taking out student loans to enroll in the program. Once these distressed people had paid their tuition money, many were immediately put back on the street. What can be said about conscience development among these grown-ups and their corporations who certainly should, and often know better?

Of course we need to be cautious before concluding that most, if not all consciences appear to be parked in neutral these days. That this isn't so is noted in the actions of executives at Hilby Wilson, Inc., a San Diego investment firm specializing in land syndication.

Action by officials at this firm restore our faith in ethics when we learn how they refused to pass off investment risks to others that they themselves were not willing to accept. Sound too good to be true --- <u>especially</u> in a tight financial market?

Believing a $2.7 million hotel in El Paso, Texas would profit from twin plants --- American companies operating firms in both the U.S. and Mexico --- Hilby Wilson purchased a downtown El Paso property, investing heavily in renovations before proceeding to market this opportunity to their clients.

After limited partnerships had been sold to several investors, Hilby Wilson discovered their operating losses far out-paced previous projections. They had simply made a mistake. It was the <u>east</u> side of El Paso, not downtown, that was attracting twin-plant companies.

Faced with a choice of ignoring their findings and proceeding ahead with plans by continuing to sell this 'opportunity' as opposed to returning investors' checks and absorbing these losses themselves, Hilby Wilson's highly developed corporate conscience prevailed.

The hotel was sold back to the bank for the price of the mortgage. Checks were returned to investors, along with letters of explanation admitting the company's mistake. Company principals then split the remaining renovation loss of $3 million, which wiped out 10 percent of the firm's assets, along with a significant portion of its principle.

Hardly a good business decision, some would say. Yet the payoff for Hilby Wilson is best observed in the subsequent outpouring of letters from clients commending the firm's honesty and expressions of confidence in its business abilities. Reported one Hilby Wilson executive, "They [the firm's clients] say they are looking forward to working with us on future deals."

An ethical decision that worked? Of course, and the long term payoff should be significant for Hilby Wilson, a company not content to limit its horizons to immediate profits.

The challenge to individuals --- whether or not payoff will result --- is best found in the question: "Are you continually conscious of the need to develop your conscience?"

You need to be vigilant in taking care that you don't fall asleep at the switch when it comes to violating your conscience --- a commodity far more valuable than anything else you will ever possess in this world, accruing not only to yourself, but to your employer, as well.

Exercise

1. Do most of the people you know follow the practice --- "Let your conscience be your guide?" What is the distinction between those who do and those who don't?

2. On a scale of 1 to 10 (from an extremely poorly developed to a highly developed conscience) how do you rate yourself?

3.   Using a similar scale, what rating would you
     assign the conscience development of those
     persons you most admire?

     Name   Circle One
     _____   1 2 3 4 5 6 7 8 9 10
     _____   1 2 3 4 5 6 7 8 9 10
     _____   1 2 3 4 5 6 7 8 9 10

     What accounts for the differences among these
     individuals?

4.   What were the most important factors leading to
     the highly ethical decisions by the executives at
     Hilby Wilson?

5.   What do you think will be the ultimate payoff for
     Hilby Wilson in this instance? How long can the
     company expect to continue benefiting from this
     action?

CHAPTER TWENTY-FOUR

"Cash Preferable in <u>all</u> Transactions?"

"Money talks --- cash whispers," so says the business wit who is also quick to proclaim, "business ethics is an oxymoron." Though this second claim is often debated in business circles, admittedly when it comes to cash transactions there is a strong temptation by many enterprisers to circumvent the law.

Investigators of the House Ways and Means oversight subcommittee discovered that of 79 businesses called on in nine cities, only three hesitated to violate a 1984 federal law requiring businesses to report to the Internal Revenue Service any cash transaction of $10,000 or more. This law was passed in part to restrict the laundering of drug payments and other tainted money from passing through legitimate businesses, a law with which the business community is well versed.

Yet, in reporting back to the subcommittee, investigators described blatant examples of illegal business practices when cash transactions were attempted. For in addition to agreeing to accept cash as payment in major transactions without reporting them, some merchants agreed to accept false names from potential customers. One antique dealer implied that not only would he accept such a cash transaction, but that he also didn't expect to pay income tax on his profit. When informed the investigators wanted to close a major real estate transaction with all cash, one real estate salesperson not only agreed to keep it quiet, but actually suggested means to further circumvent the law by using cashier checks and money orders, which by law do not have to be reported.

As further evidence of cash deals quietly passing by with but a whisper, one jeweler who had Rolex watches for sale priced at $17,408 each, acknowledged that he should report any transaction over $10,000. His suggestion to get around the law? Split the purchase into two transactions, thereby avoiding the need to report a cash purchase since neither transaction would exceed $10,000.

Nor are those in the traditional professions above being tempted to pursue similar schemes to skirt the law where payment is involved. In one instance, at the conclusion of treatment, a patient broached the subject of payment for services rendered by his doctor. Pulling out his wallet the patient said, "Doc, I know most professionals keep two sets of books so give me a 10% discount for paying cash. You don't report the income and I get a discount. It's a 'win-win' situation for both of us, what do you say?"

What would you have said had you been

the professional? Does money talk or does it silence that small voice within representing an attempt by your conscience to get you to do the right thing at or away from work?

If it is easy to do what is right when the amount of cash in question is small, what amount is required to tempt you or others in your company from taking the cash and running, hiding the transaction as best you can?

One of the problems with cash transactions is that they are difficult to trace, even when dealing with relatively small sums of money. Waiters and waitresses continually battle tax authorities to determine how much of their income is derived from tips. Because most people tip by leaving cash, it is easy to underestimate one's actual income, hence the use of formulas by the Internal Revenue Service to determine "real" income for many in the service field. Of course said formulas may be grossly unfair to some, while at the same time proving overly generous to others.

In business transactions most legitimate businesses prefer checks, not cash, in doing business that involves a large payment. This removes any stigma of wrong-doing, leaving a paper trail of the transaction that will satisfy the most ardent IRS sleuth. Further, it provides a means of allowing businesses records of their day-to-day dealings, satisfying any internal audit or potential challenges by stockholders in publicly held firms.

written receipts in exchange for payment, with firms keeping copies of each receipt, should dispel any concern of wrongdoing. Further, it underscores for all employees that this is the <u>only</u> means by which cash transactions will be handled.

Obviously with small purchases cash is sometimes more convenient.   But for the sake of avoiding future trouble from the IRS or other investigating arms of federal, state, or local governments, cash is hardly the preferred means of doing business.

Exercise

1. What legitimate reasons come to mind making cash transactions popular for many businesses?

2. Do you consider the 1984 law requiring firms to report any cash transactions of $10,000 or more to the IRS an enforceable act when a significant loophole defines cash as currency and coin, thus excluding the reporting of cashier's checks, money orders, etc.?

3. How could regulatory agencies better follow cash transactions to assure that illegally gained money is not being laundered?

4. Can a case be made that it is ever <u>immoral</u> to offer cash discounts for products or services rendered or performed?   Explain.

5. Given the opportunity, do you believe most people will underestimate income derived from cash transactions? Would you?

6. Can you think of any justifiable position for agreeing to a cash transaction about which you promised to remain quiet?

CHAPTER TWENTY-FIVE

"When Trading at Another's Expense"

Unfair advantage. Everyone knows what it is. Most can cite chapter and verse of instances where they feel they have been treated unfairly.

"Life isn't fair," it's true, but in the pursuit of doing what is right you will hardly want to compound this truism, not in your own life nor in the lives of those with whom you interact. Avoiding taking advantage of another is to choose to travel the high, not the low road. Which path do you think is most often chosen?

An automobile executive once accepted a trade of a practically worthless car on a newer model that wasn't much better. When the not too bright purchaser inquired, "How long must I make payments?," the response was, "Just make 'em 'til I tell you to stop." Trading at another's expense, while not universal in the business world, occurs often enough to give commerce a bad image in the eyes of many.

"Trading at another's expense" is usually a figurative phrase but in all too many instances it is taken literally. Not long ago a New York psychiatrist pled guilty to buying stock based on information acquired from an unwitting patient. The doctor admitted buying shares in a banking corporation after his patient, the wife of a Wall Street financier, revealed in therapy that she was worried about changes in her life if her husband's bid to buy the corporation succeeded. Trading in the stock prior to a public announcement, the physician was charged with earning thousands of dollars illegally from his access to privileged information.

Brokers face an even greater temptation of trading at another's expense. Working in a profession where earnings are nearly always tied exclusively to commissions, it is tempting to generate income simply by trading one stock issue for another. Commonly known as churning an account, i.e., where stock is bought and sold not to benefit the investor but rather to line the pocket of the broker, is a practice not unheard of in financial circles.

One stockbroker confessed that he is constantly torn between what is fair to his clients and his need to provide for his family. "Sadly," he confessed, "the client doesn't always come out on top." Though this shouldn't be the case, it is not surprising given the tempting scenario of choosing between another's and one's own self-interest in financial transactions.

Most pronounced during the last decade are the insider-trading scandals that rocked Wall Street investment firms. Michael Milken, with the Drexel

Burnham Lambert Wall Street investment firm, entered a plea bargain agreeing to several felony counts and agreed to pay over $600 million in fines and restitutions. This amounted to only somewhat more than the $550 million he had earned from Drexel --- in 1987 alone!

Charged with having manipulated stock prices, defrauding stockholders and clients, and having profited illegally in more than a dozen corporate restructures and takeovers, Milken had little choice but to make a deal. Nor was this the first case of such fiscal impropriety.

Earlier, Ivan Boesky, a former stock speculator, touched off a major Wall Street investigation when he settled an insider-trading case by paying $100 million and agreeing to cooperate with investigators. Sentenced to prison, he cooperated by testifying concerning trading by brokers at investors' expense, incriminating numerous individuals who had used their professional positions to take advantage of unwitting clients.

But Wall Street aside, any time businesses take advantage of customers by charging unconscionable prices or earning unwarranted profits, trading at the expense of another occurs. Obviously there is no set limit as to how much is too much when it comes to profits. Usually the market makes an eventual correction, reducing profits that are out of line. However, opportunities to trade at another's expense are present every day.

The pertinent question for each of us is, "Do I refrain from taking undue advantage of another whenever the opportunity arises?" And "Does this apply to company policy, as well?"

Exercise

1. What unfair advantage of others have (1) you, and (2) your company foregone in the past?

2. What case can be made for a trend toward individuals and corporations electing to take the "high" as opposed to the "low" road in business dealings?

3. How do you feel insider trading using privileged information could be best discouraged?

4.   What issues must individuals in corporate decision making positions face when deciding on ethical choices as these relate to (1) customers; (2) stockholders, and (3) employees?

5.   How effective are prison terms in quelling insider-trading by security professionals on Wall Street? Is there a better approach?

6.   In your mind, what constitutes an unconscionable profit?

7.   If given the opportunity to "make a killing" would you succumb to the temptation? Consider the consequences of your response, whether affirmative or negative.

CHAPTER TWENTY-SIX

"The Company is Responsible"

A department head invited several employees to dinner in celebration of the group's completion of a major task. When the check arrived everyone contributed cash to cover the cost of the dutch-treat meal. The supervisor then picked up the money from the table, paid the entire amount with her charge card, and later submitted the bill on her expense account.

When an underling discovered this she was deeply troubled. What was her responsibility to her boss? To the company? Indeed, to herself?

Who is ultimately responsible when a contractor falsifies test results in order to fill a contract? A bolt manufacturer faked documents to the military for nearly a decade, certifying that its bolts met government standards though only one batch of bolts had ever been tested by an outside firm. Even then the testing firm issued a report critical of the bolts. The contractor's response? Simple. Test results were falsified.

It is difficult to argue corporate responsiveness until an infraction is brought to management's attention. But once such an accusation is made there is little question but that the company is responsible for ferreting out any wrongdoing, setting exemplary examples for other employees to follow in the future.

Further, often it is a test of credulity that mass subterfuge can go on behind the backs of top management. A predominantly displayed sign on President Truman's oval office desk proclaimed, "The buck stops here", a philosophy befitting those at the helm of any organization. Why? Because ultimately, the company will be held responsible for whatever transpires in getting the job done.

Stories recently surfaced concerning allegations of coercion and extortion by a convenience-store chain. Fearing employee theft, company sleuths reportedly became overly aggressive when confronting suspected pilfers. One employee, told by a loss-prevention specialist that videotapes and photos of her stealing goods and money were on hand, was ordered to sign a statement agreeing to such charges or be taken to jail. Petrified, the employee signed a statement --- one that had been dictated to her.

On the surface it might appear that only those who are guilty or who have something to fear would be intimidated by such tactics. But given the lack of ego strengths in many, we know this isn't necessarily so. Especially in the instance at hand, where this particular employee was found to be mentally impaired.

One former loss-prevention specialist at the firm reported that he was expected to bring in at least the equivalent of his salary in confession money. Once while in the midst of interrogating one employee he said he remembered feeling "...she might be slightly retarded."

Observed another former investigator, "They're not catching the thieves. They're catching the people who are easily manipulated."

Again, who is responsible? Internal auditing within the company or the company itself? In any event, a company will be held liable and responsible for any actions taken on its behalf by employees or outside contractors. Thus it behooves every corporate head to make certain that he or she is aware of all company policies and to assure such practices are fairly implemented. This is so for two reasons.

First, it is good business to be known as a highly respected company. Not only does this cause able employees to seek work in such an environment, but it carries over to customers who through transference of a widely held belief of corporate standards will be anxious to do business with a company of such integrity when the opportunity arises.

Second, companies that have reputations for choosing the harder right over the easier wrong, for biting the bullet and making tough decisions especially when it is not to their immediate bottom line advantage are firms that will instill a strong loyalty from employees who presume they will be equally well-treated by a corporation that chooses to apply such high ethical principles to its business endeavors.

Where companies assume responsibility for whatever is done in their names, public confidence ensues, causing a bonding between the expectations of high performance and a pursuit of lofty goals. This helps forge a greater effort at all levels within the company to pursue what is right.

And though individuals may act on behalf of a company, in the final analysis it is not the individual who will be held accountable for the company's behavior but rather <u>the company</u> that will be charged with responsibility for the individual affiliate's deportment.

Exercise

1. What is a company's responsibility to an individual who has misplaced corporate trust? How far should the company bend?

2. In responding to an employee's ethical indiscretion what should the company consider regarding the affect on other employees?

3. Without encouraging "tattling", what can a company do to stimulate employees to report work place infractions before these problems become unmanageable?

4. When someone crosses the line of fairness in enforcing perceived corporate policy, what are their choices? Which are their best choices?

5. List those companies you believe have the best reputations in the business community where you live.

6. What practices do these companies follow that could be incorporated by other firms to enhance their reputations?

7. What practices can your company institute that would improve its reputation: (a) among employees, and (b) with current and potential customers?

CHAPTER TWENTY-SEVEN

"An Odyssey of Choice: Whose?"

Americans assume that no expense should be spared when it comes to health. Especially theirs. Good theory, we might agree, but is it practical?

A baby is born with serious defects. The mother having been a long-term drug abuser gives birth to an infant who is brain damaged, has no control of her arms and legs, is deaf, and whose lungs cannot sustain breathing.

For the next several months the infant is given 24-hour nursing care while exposed to multiple surgical procedures. She contracts a staph infection. At the end of the first year the child's physical condition has not improved and her medical expenses total close to one million dollars. Further, her attending physicians do not expect her condition will substantially improve.

Nor is the problem confined to the new born. Demand for health procedures and operations is already greater than what is available. Like it or not, rationing of medical procedures is upon us. At issue is not only what choices we must make but <u>who</u> will sit in judgment weighing various options so critical to the health of us all?

So far the criteria of medical practioners administering treatment or performing various diagnostic tests often entails an unspoken agreement, "When in doubt, do it." The problem is that cost is quickly becoming just as legitimate a consideration by medical administrators, government regulators, and health insurance plans.

A corollary is the old adage of doing everything possible to prolong life in nearly every case. The problem with such an approach is that not only can it lead to poor care at high cost but it is no longer supportable. Deciding when to let go or when enough is enough is not only a medical decision but one all of society must confront. For obvious reasons such decisions are usually faced first by the immediate family. But how much right does the family, or the patient for that matter, have to mandate what care should be provided?

We are only kidding ourselves when we cling to the attitude, "More is better". There is a limit not only to technology and technological advances but to collective societal resources, as well.

We have long had more patients desiring heart transplants than available organs. The same is true for kidneys and other vital body components. When these aren't available patients die. However, often the life expectancy is not substantially increased even when patients have received such transplants. What then is the answer?

Nor is the problem restricted to transplanted organs. Some oft performed surgical procedures are unnecessary. It is widely believed among scientists that many operations performed do not contribute significantly to one's lifestyle or longevity. The same is true with various other medical procedures.

For example, total parenteral nutrition (TPN) is a recently expanded technology permitting a form of tube or artificial feedings intravenously via a catheter entering a vein when patients are unable to sustain themselves via oral nourishment. Says Dr. Seymour Perry, of Georgetown University, "Take some poor fellow dying of AIDS and cachexia [emaciation caused by malnutrition]. Not much can be done, but friends or relatives see him literally starve, and a doctor may suggest TPN. There goes $500 a day [and] you're not going to prolong life very much..."

No one wants to equate health care with fiscal expenditure but realistically, "What is the alternative?" Choices must be made as to what society value's most when it comes to patient care. For even if the matter is ignored, constraints of availability of technology, to say nothing of our limited resources, will dictate choices upon demand that may be less preferable than others arrived at through more careful scrutiny.

Not only is the matter an odyssey of

choice but the question remains, "Who is best positioned to make these choices?" What do you think?

Exercise

1. Is it reasonable to assume that no expense should be spared when it comes to your loved one's health? If your answer is, "No," what limits would you impose?

2. How receptive do you think Americans will be to rationing medical procedures?

3. Who [or which institution] do you think is best equipped to decide how medical rationing should be handled?

4. How many different reasons can you think of for health practioners following medical procedures to adapt the philosophy, "When in doubt, do it"?

5. Why shouldn't the patient or immediate family have the right to mandate what care should be provided?

6. What criteria would you recommend before patients are considered for organ transplants?

CHAPTER TWENTY-EIGHT

"The Tougher Choices"

Nice guys finish _____. But before
(fill in the blank)
possibly concluding it doesn't pay to be nice, consider
evidence to the contrary.

Not only is being nice conducive to positive mental health for one exhibiting such behavior, it is also good business, paying off in countless ways. In fact, going the second mile or making the extra effort is nearly <u>always</u> good business, awarding both employees and customers or consumers.

Think of the firms with which you like to do business. Chances are that not one has a monopoly on services rendered. Your choices in deciding with whom you will do business are probably based in no small way on your perception of how a given firm treats people.

Reflecting on those businesses you patronize, how many of these do you buy from because you have been treated nicely by their employees, been impressed with their good deeds, or responsible citizenship?

At American Speedy Printing in

Tallahassee, Florida, new customers are met by George and Bev Karmanos who don't sell them printing; rather they educate them as consumers, taking customers on a tour of the plant so they understand the printing process. The payoff? By taking an interest in and showing customers how they are saving money on one job, they are more likely to return with their future business needs.

As further evidence of the "nice guy" approach paying off, the Karmanoses never let a job go out without enclosing a letter thanking the customer for placing the order. And they will rerun any job no matter who was at fault. Internal rewards are shared with employees, who enjoy generous benefits, vacations, holidays, a profit sharing pension plan, and handsome bonuses paid semi-annually.

Or consider Steve Lauer, operator of Subway Sandwiches in Fort Collins, Colorado. His employee turnover is less than 50 percent a year, far below the usual 300 percent experienced by many fast-food operations. The reasons? Scheduling is flexible, with staff free to set their hours around another job, a family priority or school. Tasks are also rotated to help prevent burnout, with bonuses and parties rewarding good work.

One of the youngest franchisees in the nation, Lauer's greatest success has been in marketing. He develops good-neighbor public-relation campaigns, helping the local youth baseball league raise money by designing a coupon book. Team managers receive a Player of the Game free-sandwich coupon to award one of their charges. In addition, anyone participating in the Great American Smokeout, the March of Dimes Walkathon, or a Red Cross blood drive, gets a coupon. Elementary school teachers also receive coupons to hand out to students who complete assigned reading lists.

Rewards for Lauer abound in word of mouth advertising bringing in a stream of new business, to say nothing of the personal satisfaction received in returning something to the community providing his income.

Business commitment and investment in a community have also paid handsome dividends for Chicago's South Shore Bank, serving the inner city by devoting its resources to financing two declining neighborhoods. The bank requires that real estate loans be used to fix up local properties in South Shore and Austin. Of interest is South Shore Bank's profits. It has generated a profit every year since 1975, while helping to create an unlikely group of entrepreneurs who specialize in rehabilitating rundown buildings. With assets of $200 million and earnings of $1.47 million in 1990, the bank has proven it can <u>do good in doing well</u>, even in lean times.

Small companies, large corporations, and even giant conglomerates have joined in active pursuit of ethics in action. In recent years the Aluminum Company of America (Alcoa) of Pittsburgh, began to reshape the company's corporate conscience with emphasis on six "core values": (1) integrity; (2) safety and health; (3) quality of work; (4) treatment of people; (5) accountability, and (6) profitability. Their goal is to become a unified and harmonious enterprise ready to compete in future global markets. Alcoa is assigned high marks by employees who praise the company for not sacrificing these values in light of the current recession. Regarding good or bad industry years, Chairman Paul H. O'Neill comments, "I don't think it's necessary to compromise your values to succeed economically." Conversely, companies will succeed precisely because of their attention to values.

A common thread running through the business culture of each of these examples is their dual interest in employees and customers, proving once again, "Nice guys don't finish last. Rather, they are more likely to finish first, as are their businesses."

Does it really pay corporations to be ethical? In a comparison of returns for companies listed with DSI (Kinder, Lydenberg, Domini and Company's common stock index of 400 U. S. companies rated for operating ethically and socially responsible) and Standard & Poor's 500 from 1986 to 1990, the return for both was similar: 80 percent. With many stockholders demanding that companies operate ethically and practice good corporate citizenship, this decade could witness many more positive changes as corporations strive to distance themselves from what has been described as a decade of greed (the 1980's), where too often the pursuit was fueled by ethics inaction. In the 1990's the emphasis is expected to focus instead on ethics in action.

Exercise

1. Why do so many Americans conclude that nice guys finish last?

2. In your personal experience have you felt nice guys finish last or first? What has helped to crystalize these thoughts?

3. What examples can you think of where being nice in business has paid handsome dividends?

4. As a business person what distinguishes being nice in customer/employee relations and "giving away the store"?

5. Can you think of business settings where following the Golden Rule, i.e., treating customers as you would want to be treated, does not work?

6. Can an employer be "too" nice to employees? Cite examples.

CHAPTER TWENTY-NINE

"Fixed Attributes of an Ethical Organization?"

The bottom line: at first glance the best objective measure of a company's performance. Right?

Well, consider what is most important: profits now or profits later? With bottom line results limited to current profitability, isn't it possible that the importance placed on present bottom line criteria could have a negative affect on future profitability?

J. C. Penney's, along with its late founder of the same name, is a case in point. At the outset of his mercantile career, James Cash Penney decided to base his business dealings on the ethic of the Golden Rule. This was to be accompanied by self-reliance, self-discipline and honor. Early success accrued from Penney's primary rule of humane and fair conduct toward both his employees and customers.

Borrowing start-up capital of $1500, he astonished his banker by announcing his envisioned "Golden Rule" chain of stores. Sales of quality clothing and dry goods were to be offered for cash and carry at prices lower than those available at the then prevalent company stores. Further, each customer's satisfaction was guaranteed, an offer heatedly debated as unheard of business orthodoxy.

By 1912 there were 34 Golden Rule stores. When the renamed J.C. Penney Company celebrated its Silver Anniversary in 1927, the chain had grown to 892 stores. Throughout the years Penney never had an "employee". Everyone was an "associate", with local store managers considered Penney's partners. In addition, each manager trained an assistant, who became a partner in that store before moving on, opening another store within the chain on his own. These three man partnerships --- the third man always being Penney --- led to the latter being known as the man with a thousand partners.

Loyalty accruing to Penney as a result of his ethical dealings with his partners became legendary. His willingness to sacrifice immediate profits on occasion in exchange for customer satisfaction through his guaranteed policy proved of incalculable value to Penney during the early years of the great depression.

Broke in 1933 at age 56, Penney was discouraged and ill in a sanitarium at Battle Creek, Michigan. After a dramatic restorative experience of his faith in God and his own will to live, Penney decided to return to the mercantile field, starting a second career.

Borrowing against a $3 million life insurance policy, he regained a stake in his old company, where stock shares had dropped from a high of 120 to a low of 13. Then the real genius of his earlier decision to treat his associates ethically paid off --- in spades!

A number of his former associates banded together, buying company stock at the depressed price and later, when the market recovered, sold these shares to Mr. Penney at the lower price. While some argue such generosity is a thing of the past, ethical corporations led by ethical leaders are anything but remnants of a former philosophical outlook.

For instance, in the modern mercantile world the west coast firm of Nordstrom's is widely recognized for its ethical conduct. Customers flock to their stores with full assurance that the company stands unequivocally behind any item it sells. With a return policy that occasionally results in financial loss for the corporation, nonetheless, the company stands firm in its commitment to deal ethically with its customers.

One woman bought a pair of shoes at Nordstrom's and six months later was in the store's shoe department looking at another shoe. Recognizing the shoes the customer was wearing, the clerk inquired how the lady liked them.

"They are very comfortable," she replied, "but in only six months the soles have worn more than I thought they would." The clerk apologized and went off. Returning with a new pair of shoes like those she was wearing, the clerk insisted the customer leave her old shoes, wearing the replacement pair home. And this though half a year had lapsed since the customer's original shoe purchase!

Certainly among the best examples of business ethics in recent years is the response of Johnson & Johnson to the 1983 Tylenol scare. Isolated reports of contaminated bottles of the product causing person's deaths put immediate financial pressure on the company. A containment approach, identifying the problem as a local one and recalling the product in that sole area must have been tempting. However, without hesitation and at great financial sacrifice, J&J ordered the entire product pulled from shelves around the country. Some analysts wondered if the company, never mind the product, would survive.

Today we know the rest of the story, for J&J is recognized as a leader almost without peer in the business world, admired for its ethical commitment of doing what's right --- especially when the choice is difficult. Indeed, both the company and its newly formulated product enjoy greater prestige than ever, none of which would be possible had there not been an action oriented commitment to ethics from the top down.

Can there be any doubt in the effectiveness of adhering to the highest order of ethics for the long term good of a company? Truly it's a thought worth considering.

Exercise

1. In what ways can short-term emphasis on the bottom line have a negative affect on future profitability?

2. Why do you think the practice of following the "Golden Rule", i.e., doing unto others as you would want others to do unto you, is so seldom actively applied in the pursuit of business?

3. In addition to the companies cited here as ethical corporations, what additional firms come to mind as businesses operating with a definite code of ethics? What examples can you cite?

4.   In the long run is it better for a company, such as
      Nordstrom's, to position itself ethically, even if this
      means being taken advantage of occasionally by
      an unethical customer? Why?

5.   From what you consider least effective to most
      effective, rank order the possibilities J&J faced in
      1983 with its Tylenol product crisis.

6.   Once confronted with the Tylenol crisis described
      above, what response would you have
      recommended had you been a J&J executive at
      the time?

CHAPTER THIRTY

"Choosing the Harder Right over the Easier Wrong"

Individuals frequently feel confronted with a choice between (1) the harder right and (2) the easier wrong, when many times the more accurate perception should be that of the <u>harder wrong</u> versus the <u>easier right</u>. For often what seems such an easy choice at first may prove to have been anything but.

Examples abound in business where some maintain you can't afford to be too honest. Unfortunately there are those who readily agree with such an assertion.

At a major automotive dealership in Houston, dozens of locals allegedly bought new cars, yet never made a payment. The manager of the dealership suspected that some of his salesmen referred these customers to "credit doctors", who would alter their credit ratings in order to qualify them for a car loan. As a result of said scam, this one dealership faced a loss of $1 million dollars in missing and depreciated cars.

Nor is faking credit an ethics issue

confined to the automotive industry. Last year a real estate broker in one large city was charged with theft when he allegedly used stolen credit histories to purchase 13 foreclosed homes with VA mortgages totaling almost $1 million dollars. The broker and his confederates later sold these homes at higher prices. They were discovered when someone whose credit had been falsely used complained of credit alterations.

Or imagine that you are in sales selling high price furs. In walks a young person, whom you presume to be well under the age of 21. He inquires about a purchase, then reaches into his pocket, pulling out $25,000 --- in cash! You have to wonder where a kid this young got that kind of money. But just as you are about to inquire, another thought races through your mind: "Who cares where he got the money? In any event, if he doesn't buy from me he'll buy from someone else." Such is the way we soothe our consciences when faced with choosing what <u>seems</u> to be the harder right over the easier wrong.

None of the answers in any of these instances is as simple as it might first seem. Theoretically it is easy to come down on the side of what is right ethically, at least in most instances. But talking about and acting on ethical choices are not one and the same.

Simply put, ethics must be both <u>taught</u> and <u>caught</u>. This means that in the work place employees must tackle ethical dilemmas so that workers continually think and talk about tough situations. Written codes of ethics, admirable though they are, are no substitute for frank discussions alerting employees to corporate ethical obligations concerning customers, stockholders, suppliers, their own colleagues, and/or the community at large.

Of course the main responsibility for establishing an ethical base rests with the CEO of a corporation or head of an agency or institution. That person is charged with making ethics an acceptable topic of conversation, for in so doing the message is sent that not only is it o.k., but expected that employees will vocalize ethical concerns. Such input from individual employees will help keep a company true to its mission, i.e., that of running an ethical business.

Few frauds start with an overt, intentional act of wrongdoing. Rather, most often fraud is the product of a combustible mixture, including unrealistic profit pressures, weak controls, bonus-heavy compensation plans, and finally an apathetic board of directors.

Even should wrongful actions go undetected, such acts prey on the consciences of perpetrators, exacting a toll that underscores the truism, i.e., it's not the harder right versus the easier wrong, but rather in the final analysis a case of <u>the harder wrong versus the easier right</u>.

Surely the Golden Rule is one helpful analytical technique to be used when making ethical choices, as is the so-called mirror test, i.e., "How would you feel about explaining a particular action to those you love most?" Your spouse? Your children? Your mother?

Exercise

1. What past decisions can you recall where you exercised the "harder wrong" rather than the "easier right"?

2. Why do we so often fall victim to the "harder wrong" in our decision making?

3. Is it possible to be <u>too</u> honest in business? What examples support your position?

4. How much influence should the argument, "If he doesn't buy from me he will from someone else," carry were you selling an item to someone of questionable resources?

5. In thinking back over the years it has taken for you to acquire your own code of ethics, have ethical teachings been more influential when "caught" or "taught"?

6. What do you think is most important to include in a written code of ethics?

7.   Can you envision a better ethical yardstick than to imagine just prior to every decision, "How would I feel about explaining this particular action to the one(s) I love most?" Substantiate your position.

SUMMARY

The Right Thing --- choosing to do what's right is a journey, based largely on two premises: (1) what you believe about yourself, and (2) what you believe about others. These two beliefs are seldom constant, lending credence to the assertion that integrity is seldom a constant in life. Rather, choices are made based upon what is perceived to be right at a given moment using all available information at hand.

Obviously most of us would like to live in a world where people with highly developed consciences choose to do what is right as they understand the right. All the time. The trouble is that far more than semantics is involved here.

It was Ogden Nash who wrote, "There is only one way to achieve happiness on this terrestrial ball, and that is to have either a clear conscience or none at all." But such a tongue-in-cheek implication aside, the only way to achieve true happiness is to work at possessing as clear a conscience as possible.

This is accomplished only when we cease to be discouraged when thinking about how many people are shocked by honesty and how few by deceit. For in a very real sense life is what we make it ethically --- day by day.

Ethics, then, is the study of how life may be full, rich and abundant; not, as often imagined, how it can be constrained, made unhappy and meager.

Giving more than casual pursuit to the preceding chapters and having examined each in light of the criteria contained in Appendix B will position you better to make choices in the future that will leave you strengthened in character as you strive to do what's right.   For this involves conscious decision making, wherein we approach life trying to do what's right, especially when it's difficult.

Finally, take heart in the sage advice of Thoreau, who adjured us to "Be not merely good; be good for something."   This we can do best when remembering John Stuart Mills' admonition that one may cause evil to others not only by his actions, but by his inactions, as well.

By pursuing what is right in both your thinking and actions you will be well on your way to being good for something special in a world that will increasingly place a higher premium on the ethical choices we are each called upon to make when we do The Right Thing.

- end -

APPENDIX A

A brief description of selected ethical styles:

1. <u>Deontological</u> or nonconsequentialism holds that ethical theories are not based on consequences but on some other moral standard. Opposite of utilitarian [see below].

2. <u>Duty</u> ascribed to Immanuel Kant's system of ethics. Kant stressed that moral acts are performed from a sense of duty, not one's inclination.

3. <u>Egoistic</u> suggests that everyone ought to act in his own self-interest.

4. <u>Hedonistic</u> holds that pleasure or happiness is the one intrinsic good or value in life. An action is moral if it brings the greatest amount of pleasure or happiness with the least amount of pain or unhappiness.

5. <u>Humanistic</u> refers to a nonreligious view of life, advocating a morality which excludes religion or religious belief.

6.   <u>Relativism</u> is the opposite of "absolutism", claiming that there are no absolutes in morality. Everyone must decide his or her own values, relative --- if at all --- to particular cultures, groups, or other individuals.

7. <u>Situational</u> claims no moral rules or guides except for Christian love. The loving thing to do in any situation --- that is the moral thing to do.

8. <u>Utilitarian</u> is a normative ethical theory advocating bringing about good consequences or happiness to all concerned. Sometimes stated as the greatest good for the greatest number.

APPENDIX B

<u>Six Point Test for Deciding Right from Wrong</u>

Apply the following test based on the late Dr. Harry Emerson Fosdick's ethical criteria to your decision making as you reflect on ethical choices as presented in each chapter. Such an exercise will not only assist you with these specific ethical decisions but should prove invaluable in assisting you when confronting future ethical choices.

1. Does your chosen course of action seem logical and reasonable? Forget what others might say. Does it make sense to you? If so, it is probably right.

2. Does the solution you choose pass the test of sportsmanship? Or to state it otherwise, if everyone followed this same course of action, would the results be beneficial for all?

3. Where do you think your plan of action will lead? What affect will it have on others? What affect will it have on you?

4. How well will you think of yourself when you look back at what your have done?

5. Separate yourself from the problem. Imagine it is a problem affecting the person you most admire. How would that person respond to this problem?

6. What difference would it make if everyone knew about your decision? Especially consider how you would feel if your family members and friends knew what you have done or plan to do. Chances are decisions made in hopes that no one will find out are not ethical.

ANNOTATED BIBLIOGRAPHY

Colen, B. D.<u>Hard Choices: Mixed Blessings of Modern Medical Technology</u>. New York: G. P. Putnam's Sons, 1986.

Examines major ethical dilemmas arising from applying modern medical technology. Case histories allow in-depth examination of in vitro fertilization, keeping infants alive in intensive care nurseries, and the enormous financial and ethical problems surrounding organ transplants.

Fletcher, Joseph. <u>Situation Ethics: The New Morality</u>. Philadelphia: The Westminster Press, 1966.

In an attempt to extricate modern man from rigid, archaic rules and codes within an ethic of love, an outline is presented for decision-making, presupposing individual responsibility. Controversial are the ideas that everyone must decide for himself what is right and that <u>any</u> act <u>could</u> be right, depending on the circumstances.

Hodges, Luther H.   <u>The Business Conscience</u>. Englewood Cliffs, N.J.: Prentice-Hall, Inc., 1963.

> A former Secretary of Commerce examines the moral and ethical problems in business, recognizing that though ethical principles remain constant over long periods, situations change. Of relevance to students, parents, government officials and members of the business community.

Jones, W. T., Frederick Sontag, Morton O. Beckner, and Robert J. Fogelin (eds.). <u>Approaches to Ethics. Representative Selections from Classical Times to the Present</u>. New York: McGraw-Hill Book Company, Inc., 1962.

> An anthology presenting major ethical theories from classical to the present era. Continues to serve as a primary source book for ethics discussions at every stage, with selections of varying levels of difficulty challenging the casual to the serious student of the subject.

Liebig, James E. <u>Business Ethics: Profiles in Civic Virtue</u>. Golden, Colorado: Fulcrum Publishing, 1990.

Twenty-four case studies of individuals and the companies they head, e.g., Control Data, Hammermill Paper Company, The Hanover Insurance Companies, Republic Airlines and Texas Utilities Generating Company, are examined to discern the dramatic effect of their views on business ethics. Conclusion: the virtuous leader is alive and well.

Macklin, Ruth. <u>Mortal Choices: Bioethics in Today's World</u>. New York: Pantheon Books, 1987.

A thought-provoking review of the dilemma pitting what is medically possible against what is morally desirable. Thought provoking issues are considered such as who can decide how much treatment is enough and what happens when patient's rights conflict with the will of those around them?

Macniven, Don (ed.). Moral Expertise: Studies in Practical and Professional Ethics. London: Routledge, 1990.

> Views ethical issues from a feminist (care and personal responsibility) to a masculine (abstract, rationalistic and concerned with rules of fair play) perspective. An ethical update addressing issues affecting human reproduction, planetary engineering, the environment, and the interplay with social science, provide a bridge from ethics in the present to ethics in the future.

Solomon, Robert C. and Kristine R. Hanson. It's Good Business. New York: Atheneum, 1985.

> Explores how a workable ethics program can save a company when disaster strikes. Suggestions and exercises for putting such a program in place at virtually any kind of company are offered. Analyses can be used and worked repeatedly by business people in multiple types of business settings.

Walton, Clarence C. <u>The Moral Manager</u>. Cambridge, Massachusetts: Ballinger Publishing Company, 1988.

Examines bedrock values of business professionals' decisions and actions, including relevance of moral character to managerial effectiveness; how virtue is instilled, and how to maintain those organizational values that brought about success. "Value quizzes" at outset of each chapter challenge readers' belief systems as applied to the complexity of waiting ethical dilemmas.

INDEX

About the Author

William D. Brown is a clinical psychologist in private practice in Washington, D.C. A syndicated newspaper columnist for more than a decade, he is also the author of <u>Families Under Stress</u> (Wycliff, 1977) and <u>Welcome Stress! it can help you be your best</u> (CompCare, 1983).

A prolific writer, his articles have appeared in both professional and popular publications, including the <u>Los Angeles Times Syndicate</u> and the <u>National Business Employment Weekly</u> of the <u>Wall Street Journal</u>, among many others.

Dr. Brown speaks and conducts seminars on ethics and stress for Fortune 500 corporations and major associations around the country. A partial speaking client list includes the American Bankers Association, American College of Physicians, Bell Atlantic, Marriott and General Foods.

Bill and his wife of more than 30 years have two grown children.

Call 1-800-886-0860
to order additional copies of

The Right Thing

ethics • **ethics**
inaction **in action**

at $12.95 a copy. Add $2.00 for shipping and handling.
Please have credit card information ready.

Or clip and mail this form to:

The Wayne Smith Company
1300 L Street, N.W., Suite 1050
Washington, DC 20005

Name _____

Address _____

City/State/Zip _____

****

Method of payment: [check one]
_____ Personal/corporate check
_____ Money Order
_____ American Express ____ MasterCard ____Visa

Credit Card Account # _____
Expiration Date _____
Signature _____

{Please allow 3 weeks for shipment}